the CHAMPAGNE GANG

the CHAMPAGNE GANG

HIGH TIMES AND SWEET CRIMES

Jeremy Mercer

Warwick Publishing
Toronto Los Angeles

ISBN: 1-895629-97-7

Published by:
Warwick Publishing Inc., 388 King Street West, Suite 111, Toronto, Ontario M5V 1K2
Warwick Publishing Inc., 1424 N. Highland Avenue, Los Angeles, CA 90027

Distributed by:
Firefly Books Ltd., 3680 Victoria Park Avenue, Willowdale, Ontario M2H 3K1

Cover Design: Kimberley Young
Book Design: Diane Farenick
Editorial Services: Melinda Tate
Photographs courtesy of Jeremy Mercer, except for front cover, bottom pic courtesty of First Light

Printed and bound in Canada

Acknowledgements

First, I would like to thank James Williamson and Warwick Publishing for taking a chance on a young writer for this project. They have been nothing but professional in their dealings and an author could ask for nothing more from his publisher.

For those at the *Ottawa Citizen* who gave me both my start in the business and the time to work on this book, I also extend my gratitude. To Tina Spencer and Keri Sweetman, for their early and continued support and encouragement. To Don Campbell, a grizzled veteran of the police beat, thanks for showing me the ropes. To Barb Petek, who even read unfinished chapters during her cottage vacation.

To Klaus Pohle, who opened his heart and his office at the Carleton School of Journalism to this young writer, some fine cigars are coming his way.

I would also like to thank all those who took their time with me and provided the information vital to this book, especially Det. Staff Sgt. Glen Bowmaster and his partner Det. Const. Mike Fagan of the Ontario Provincial Police, who endured countless questions over beer — off duty, of course — at The Prescott with incredible patience.

And then there is the gang themselves: Kevin Grandmaison, Yves Belanger, Marc Flamini and Tyler Wilson. Without their co-operation, this book would not have been possible. They humoured me during my countless jail visits and the endless phone calls I needed to iron out the smallest details of their story.

To my parents, Ross and Patricia, and my friends, especially Kate Ready, who helped me get through these exhausting months, well, what else can I say: I owe them much.

And finally, a special thanks goes out to Dave Ebner, a Carleton University journalism student who took so many precious hours of his summer to help edit, shape and critique the manuscript. Without his enthusiasm and innovation, this book never would have been the same. I look forward to reading his first novel.

Jeremy Mercer

Author's Note

The characters and events described in this book are real, but it bears mentioning that I have used pseudonyms for a number of them who have yet to be prosecuted by the courts or for whom privacy is a consideration. In several circumstances, I have even gone a step further and altered their descriptions. None of the main characters have been affected by these changes.

Though this is a work of non-fiction, I have taken certain storytelling liberties, particularly with the sequence of events for the sake of the book's narrative.

Where the book strays from straight non-fiction, my intention has been to remain faithful to the characters and to the events as they unfolded.

Chapter ONE

February 14, 1996
St. Catharines, Ontario

An icy winter rain was beating hard against the bathroom window when Kevin Grandmaison stepped out of the shower. He grabbed one of the coarse hotel towels, wiped the steam away from the window, and then stood up onto the toilet to get a good look outside. Damn.

It was dark, real dark, with no moon in the February sky. From the lights of the hotel, Kevin could see the gleaming ice beginning to clot against the trees and coat the cars in the parking lot below. He pressed his forehead against the cold window pane and stared past the trees into the downtown lights of St. Catharines where his night's work awaited him. Damn.

Kevin lowered himself from the window and sat down on the porcelain toilet, burying his face in his knees. He had to think.

The freezing rain was bad. If everything iced up, it was going to make tonight's job harder, no doubt about it. But it wasn't just the prospect of having to climb icy pipes that worried him. The rain was a sign. Yet another bad sign.

He wasn't that superstitious. Fuck that. But he had been in the game long enough to know when someone was trying to tell him something. And this time they were shouting. Over and over again.

The whole trip, ever since the crew — him, Yves Belanger, Marc Flamini and Tyler Wilson — left Ottawa on Friday, things just hadn't been going right. Hell, thought Kevin, be honest. It had been a total disaster.

It was supposed to be a joke of a trip. Three easy scores in five days, scoped out and ready to go. They were simple roof jobs, the kind the gang had done more than a hundred times in the last two years. All told, the guys figured they would clear at least $200,000 on the trip, more than enough to pay off their debts and lay low for a good long while. But it just hadn't worked out that way. It was Tuesday and they still hadn't earned a dime. Now it was raining.

Kevin winced.

The first job was supposed to have been Friday night in Kingston at the Shoppers Drug Mart on Gardiners Road. They had arrived in Kingston early, maybe 6 p.m., so they had hit Stages for dinner and some drinks until it got late enough to work. No one was worried because Kevin and Yves had been in town the week before to check out the store and what kind of security systems they had inside. There were only the basics — the doors were wired and there were some motion detectors on the store floor. They could cut through those in less than five minutes. The Shoppers was going to be a piece of cake.

When they got to the drug store just before 1 a.m., it was set up just like Kevin and Yves had promised. Single-story building, part of a strip mall on a quiet street that was deserted that late at night. It was ripe to be hit.

Except for the clerks.

As he sat there in the hotel bathroom, Kevin smiled as he thought of this absurd stroke of bad luck. Of all the nights of the year to do an inventory, the Shoppers Drug Mart had to do theirs that exact Friday night. The four of them sat in their rented red Pontiac Sunbird for two hours and watched the dopey clerks wander up and down the aisles counting bottles of shampoo and sticks of deodorant. There was nothing the guys could do. When they finally packed it up and drove back to the hotel, even all the clubs were closed. They were forced to raid the mini-bar and wait for the next job.

They were supposed to head to Orillia on the Saturday, but that was a bust. Hangovers, and a couple hours of bad afternoon TV blew the day. Instead, Sunday morning they were up early, just before noon, and drove the 300-odd miles to Orillia for the second job. With Marc driving, they'd made the trip in two and a half hours. The guy always insisted on driving and never went slower than 100 mph, even if they had a trunk-load of money and stamps. Marc was a maniac.

Orillia had always been good to them. In the past couple of years they'd done a half-dozen scores in the small town and it had always been easy. In fact, the target for Sunday night, another Shoppers Drug Mart, they had hit just last June and walked away with more than $40,000.

The plan for Sunday night was supposed to be simple. The Shoppers stores, like most major drug stores, never do bank drops on the weekend, so all of Friday and Saturday's receipts would be in the safe. That money, plus their floats, which Kevin guessed would be about $50,000 in all, would be there for the taking. When you counted in the stamps, traveller's cheques and lottery tickets that they could take and resell back in Ottawa at 50 per cent of the face value, it was sizing up to be one sweet score. At least $75,000. Sunday night was the crew's favourite time to work.

That job had gone smoothly enough, at least until they were inside. Since their hit last June, the owners had installed motion detectors in the manager's office. No problem. Marc Flamini could get past motions faster than he could twist the cap off a beer. Usually. Sunday night, for some unknown reason, one of the alarms went off.

Unknown reason.

Kevin spat on the bathroom floor. Marc screwed up, that was the unknown reason. Hadn't been paying attention, and as he crawled under it his ass was too high in the air and set one off. His mind wasn't there.

It was a silent alarm, but thank God Kevin had heard the tell-tale click of the alarm being triggered. They had jumped out the back door of the drug store, which set off the main alarm system. With bells screeching the guys had torn out of the mall's parking lot and were a couple of blocks away by the time they first heard the sirens arriving at the Shoppers. They had dodged a bullet, but still had no cash.

Sunday night's mishap had shaken Kevin. Bad. He tried not to show it. But it did, like a red stamp on his forehead. All the guys were getting jumpy.

They were supposed to head to St. Catharines for the third score on the Monday, but to try and settle down, the gang took the day off. They drove down through Hamilton and Brantford to check out some potential jobs for the future and then stopped at the Brantford Canadian Tire to buy tools to replace the ones they had left in Orillia when the job went sour. The afternoon and evening were spent at a club in Toronto. The huge bar, usually packed with drunken and drugged 20-somethings on the weekend, was empty. Kevin drank $4 beers, didn't talk, and waited for Sunday's bad memories to fade into an alcohol-induced haze. He had promised himself that the St. Catharines job the next night would be better.

Y Y Y

Kevin groaned and lifted his head so he could look out the bathroom window again. Still raining. So far nothing was getting better.

He could hear the TV going loudly in the other room. Sportsline was over and the guys had it on Letterman. He thought he could hear Eddie Murphy's voice, but wasn't sure.

Kevin started to dry himself off. He hated these small-ass Howard Johnson towels. He hated Howard Johnson's period, especially this one out by the highway. It was full of truckers and didn't even have a restaurant or a bar. Normally the guys would have gotten a suite at Embassy Suites near the university, but now money was becoming a problem. The whole thing was falling apart.

In all they maybe had a couple of thousand in cash among them, plus whatever they had stashed away back in Ottawa. Not even enough to take care of an emergency. If the heat came down, they couldn't even take off for a couple of weeks.

This was a definite problem.

Kevin sighed. He hated thinking about money. He did some quick math in his head, adding up his debts for the thousandth time. Not good. Like always, the figure he arrived at was $40,000, all to bookies. He had been on a losing streak since Christmas. He hadn't won a single bet during the NFL playoffs. It was his worst run in years. To top it off, he had dropped $20,000 on the Super Bowl alone by betting the Cowboys and the over. Fucking Dallas didn't cover the spread and he had lost the whole bundle.

He needed the money this weekend for sure. Big Pino, Kevin's long-time bookie, already had his Corvette as collateral. The bastard. He was Pino's best customer and he still took the car. The guy had no compassion. Kevin knew Yves was in bad shape too, probably down $25,000.

Kevin blew his nose hard into the towel and tossed it into the bathtub. They really needed the money, or else they wouldn't even consider going out tonight.

First, there were the screw-ups at the other two jobs. That was bad karma. There was the rain — another bad sign. Then there was the heat from police. That was the worst sign of all.

When they'd been driving around St. Catharines that afternoon, Kevin was sure there was a car following them. He could have been paranoid, and the other guys didn't notice anything, but it was enough to get him worried.

The guys all figured the police knew something. They had been at the game too long and had had too many narrow escapes for the police not to be close. But Kevin still couldn't quite figure out how close.

Two weeks ago, Yves's uncle, Mike Mainville, had taken them aside for a little talk. The guy had plenty of cop friends, both in the Ontario Provincial Police and with the local police force in Ottawa.

"I'm not asking any questions, boys. What you do with your time is your business," the old, bald man told them. He had invited them over to his Vanier apartment where they sat watching a Leafs game and drinking quarts of Blue.

"But I'm just telling you — think about taking a vacation for a couple of months, or just putting your feet up and watching TV. You don't want to be working too hard, or too much, if you know what I mean."

Mike was a good man, a practical Northern Ontario man carved from the hard rock of the Canadian Shield. After the four of them had left his apartment, it was agreed they should take a sabbatical. Mike had pretty solid police connections, so there was probably something up.

Mainville's warning wasn't the only sign of police trouble. Kevin had noticed strange clicks and echoes on his phone for the past couple of weeks, especially since the meeting with Yves's uncle. He was sure police were listening in. The other guys had noticed it too. Everyone was acting on the premise that their phones and apartments were bugged.

Then there was Tyler and Marc's little problem. The two had been pinched in British Columbia three months ago, taken down for a job at a Shoppers. The case was weak, they weren't caught in the act, there was no evidence, and the guys were confident they would beat it. Still, Kevin wondered if word had filtered down to Ontario and maybe the cops were finally connecting the dots and planning to take them down.

It you took it all together, it was a big red stop sign, bathed in bright winter light.

They just wanted to do one last trip. Make that *needed* to do one last trip. After leaving Mainville's, they had agreed on a plan. There were the debts they wanted to pay down, of course. But there was also the question of living money. Not one of them had held a job in the past four years and while some of their girlfriends worked, it certainly wasn't enough coin to support the crew. If they were to take a break, and they figured six months would be enough to ice any heat that was on them, they would need enough money to pay the rent and put beer in the fridge. Not to mention a trip or two down to Mexico.

So they planned one last trip, one last hurrah. Three cake jobs in Kingston, Orillia and St. Catharines, all easy in, easy out, and they'd be set. As long as they made sure that no one was following them out of Ottawa, they'd be fine. Even if the police were close, there was no way they could know what jobs the crew had lined up in what cities.

The cardinal rule from Day One was no one outside of the four-man crew would know where they were going to hit. The only way the cops could find out was if one of them talked. And Kevin knew no one would talk. They were solid.

Even the phone taps — if they were there — didn't bother Kevin that much. In their five years together, it was the second cardinal rule — never discuss business on the phone. And they hadn't.

So they left Ottawa on Friday afternoon, confident that when they rolled back into town the next Wednesday, on Valentine's Day as it happened, they would be flush and worry-free for the next six or seven months. It had seemed like such a sure thing when they had left town. Now nothing was sure.

Kevin looked out the window again. He had the jitters. He needed to make a decision. Should they risk it and go out tonight? Or should they just pack it in and head back to Ottawa?

The guys would follow along with whatever he chose. The crew didn't really have leader, but if you had to name one, he was it.

He was the oldest at 28. The other guys were only in their early 20s. He'd been doing jobs longer than anyone and he was the one with the connections to sell off the stamps and lottery tickets. Kevin turned away from the window and looked into the bathroom mirror. He frowned. Right now, he didn't feel like a leader. His short black hair was slicked back with water and as he peered at himself, Kevin could swear his hairline was receding. His eyes were red and tired, like two pissholes in the snow as his grandfather used to say. Thin lines had been cropping up around his eyes too, a stark reminder that his thirtieth birthday was less than two years away. It was the stress, the drinking, the late nights. Then there was his body. He had worked out religiously for the past 10 years, but ever since last fall, he had started to let it lapse. His chest looked saggy, not the hard rock it once was. He weighed 205 pounds now, 25 pounds heavier than two or three years ago when he was in his prime.

He rubbed his finger over his left nipple, grimacing in pain as he pressed down on the swollen tissue. He had been having problems with his glands the past couple of years, courtesy of the steady diet of steroids he had used when he was younger to help sculpt his body. The drugs had hardened his flesh, sure, but they had also jacked up his body's production of estrogen, which had formed painful pockets around his nipples. They were known as bitch tits in weightlifting circles and most guys who were on the juice had operations to remove the glands from their chest to avoid the embarrassment. Kevin needed to look into that. Later, though. Once his work was done and he had some time to recover from the surgery, hopefully on some beach down south.

He quickly finished drying and then pulled on his work clothes: black sweatpants, a black turtle neck and black Nikes. He then piled his other clothes, his Tommy Hilfiger sweater and Calvin Klein khakis, into a plastic bag.

The last thing he did was pick up his pager, a special Sports Ticker model, and clip it to his pants. He paid $30 a month for a service that sent updated sports scores to the pager every seven minutes. It was a small price to pay so he could keep track of the games he had money on. Tonight there was a full slate of hockey games and he had bet $1,500 on four of them, straight to win. If all four turned out, he would win $4,500. The two early games, the Rangers and Flyers and the Bruins and the Blues, had both turned out in Kevin's favour, with the Flyers and Bruins cruising to victories. The other two games were on the west coast and were still in the second period. He needed the Kings to beat the Sabres and the Canucks to drop the Oilers and he would be one happy man. So far the Kings and Sabres were scoreless, but the Canucks were 2-1 on the Oilers. Maybe his luck would hold. With the pager in place he checked himself out again in the mirror.

He was ready to go.

Kevin gripped the edge of the sink and leaned into the mirror so his nose nearly brushed the glass.

They couldn't let rain stop them. If they had a tail on them, why weren't they taken down when things turned bad inside the Orillia Shoppers? The bottom line was they needed the money. There was no choice.

The night's job was on, they'd get enough to pay back the money they owed and that'd be it. It was a simple job.

Kevin smiled into the mirror. They could do this.

Besides. They were the best.

Y Y Y

The guys were still watching Letterman when Kevin came out from the bathroom. He glanced at the TV. It wasn't Eddie Murphy, but that Chris Rock guy from *Saturday Night Live*. He wasn't funny.

"About time, Kev. What were you doing? Wanking?" teased Yves, who was lying on one of the room's double beds.

Kevin didn't say a thing. Instead, he crossed the room to look out the balcony and get a better view of the freezing rain. He opened the sliding glass door and touched the railing. It was cold and wet, but not slick with ice. And the rain was beginning to peter out. This was good. Maybe they wouldn't have to climb icy pipes after all.

"Shut the fucking door," shouted Marc, who was stomach-down on the other bed. "My balls are going to freeze off."

Kevin still didn't say anything, stepped back into the room and slid the balcony door closed behind him.

He looked around the room.

Everyone was dressed the same way, in the black sweats and black shoes.

Crouched on the floor in front of the television was Tyler Wilson, probably his best friend in the group. He was a tall, almost six feet, rangy guy who kept his dark hair short and slicked back, a preppy look at helped him land the women. The nice thing about Tyler was that he was probably the quietest one of the four, not always wearing his heart on his sleeve or mouthing off. It was a wonderful contrast to Yves and Marc, who went hard all the time and usually at maximum volume. It was no surprise. At 25, Tyler was closer to Kevin's age and was a bit more mature than the other two guys. As if to prove the point, Tyler was the only one working, while Yves and Marc lounged on the beds. Wearing yellow dish-washing gloves so he would leave no fresh fingerprints, Tyler was carefully wiping down the screwdrivers, picks and other tools they would need for tonight's job.

Tyler and Kevin had started out together, and even though he was a good guy to have inside the store with you, he unfortunately couldn't crack the safes or disable the motion detectors as fast as Yves or Marc could. For that reason, Tyler always played the role of the six-man — the guy who stayed on the roof and kept an eye out for police, security guards or insomniac managers who felt like coming into the drug store at 3 a.m. to catch up on the payroll accounting. He was good at that work. The best. No one was as resourceful, and he had saved their hides a dozen times.

Tyler was the smartest too, he'd even done a year at Carleton University. With Marc and Yves so gung-ho all the time, Tyler acted as a counter-balance. He was naturally cautious and thought things out.

Over on the closest bed, Yves Belanger was checking out the hotel pay-per-view movie guide.

"Hey Kev — how about a quick look at Erotic Nights before we go, eh? Come on!"

Yves.

He had the biggest mouth of anyone, always talking, always getting on someone's nerves. It was like he had amphetamines running through his veins; he was always jumping around or acting hyper. He was a short, stocky guy, with a body like a bulldog, all coiled muscle waiting to be unleashed.

The kid was only 22, but the best guy in the world to go drinking or working with. He'd stick by you no matter what. One time when they had been out working in Vancouver, Marc had pissed off about three dozen members of the East Indian community by grabbing one of their girlfriends. Several times. Next thing you knew, they were all in the parking lot, looking for a little blood justice. Yves started whaling away on two of them, brought them both down. Then he reached into his pants and screamed, "Next one who moves get shot." Of course, he had no gun, but it stopped the other guys in their tracks. They were able to escape back into their car and were gone. No question. Yves was a good guy to have as a friend.

And to work with. He was strong enough that he could do a lot of the physical work, whether it be moving the safes or busting through a roof. With his short, squat body he was perfect for the work. He was good at breaking safes too, could crack almost as many models as Kevin.

Dressed all in black, he looked pretty intimidating, not the type of guy you'd want to meet in a dark alley after midnight. He kept his curly brown hair short and his gray eyes seemed to flicker with menace. In truth, if you were his friend, he was the sweetest guy in the world, lending you money or buying your mom things just out of the blue. And no matter how menacing he looked, the second he smiled, his harsh image was shattered. With his big goofy grin, he looked like he should be out helping old ladies cross the street, not preparing for a massive break-and-enter.

Yves was joking around now, laughing it up, but he had been jittery the last little while. He thought every second car was undercover cops and was even threatening not to go out tonight. But he was dressed and cracking jokes, thought Kevin. It was a good sign. The good signs were far and few between, and Kevin searched them out like a hard-luck gambler.

Over on the other bed was Marc Flamini, or Pretty Boy as Yves called him. Marc was also 22, and a really solid guy — but the most arrogant man Kevin had ever met. The thing that really pissed Kevin off was Marc had good reason to be cocky. The guy was a looker, with sharp blue eyes, brown hair that always had blond streaks from his countless trips south and a perpetual tan which was owed to the beaches and the dozen or so tanning clubs he had memberships in. He knew he was a looker too, pausing in front of every mirror and glass window to check his hair and admire his smooth features.

Unlike Kevin and Yves, Marc shunned the weights but still had a good physique, with cords of muscle like a swimmer. He never had any fat on him, though, and you could even call him a bit thin for his height — he was just over 5 feet 10 inches. This is something Kevin could never figure out. Marc ate out every single day, usually spending lunch and dinner in some of Ottawa's best restaurants. If for some bizarre reason Marc decided to stay in, he would cook up a storm, his Italian blood shining through as he prepared extravagant pasta and fish dishes. But despite all the food, the kid never gained a pound. It was unbelievable.

And then there were his clothes. With all the money coming in, all four of them liked their clothes — Calvin, Hilfiger, Sung, Boss. But Marc, his wardrobe was his biggest vanity. He must have spent two or three grand a month buying clothes just to impress women. His closet was unbelievable. And the guy would take care of them too, ironing everything, even his jeans. Hell, the guy could spend an hour on a single pair of khakis, just to make sure he got the creases and pleats just right. It was his obsession.

It worked too. How many times had Marc bet Kevin $1,000 that he could walk out of a bar with any woman Kevin picked out? Marc was good. Kevin ended up paying him every time, including that night in Peterborough when Kevin had singled out the short, runty, feminist bitch with glasses as Marc's prey for the night. She was in Women's Studies or some crap at Trent University and was ranting on about misogyny or some other thing. But fucking Marc had gone home with her anyway, taking Kevin's money and laughing the whole time.

"Hey," he said, telling the tale to the guys the next morning. "I just thought of Kevin's sweet ass the whole time."

Bastard.

Marc was almost as good with alarms as he was with women. He could walk into a store during the day, identify the system, spot all the motion detectors and come up with a plan of attack. Sometimes, when he was really on, Marc could even knock out the motions during store hours.

Of course he fucked up Sunday, costing them 50 or 60 dimes.

Kevin sighed.

Still, it was the best crew he had ever worked with. They had known each other for years now, having gone to the same high school, hung around the same crowds, grown up in the same neighbourhoods in Ottawa's west end. And he had never been on a run like this. They had started working together five years ago and for the last four had been working pretty steadily. They did at least four or five jobs a month, whatever it took to make sure they had enough spending money. A couple of months ago, Kevin had sat down and tried to figure out how much the gang had scored in the five years. Too much. He'd stopped counting at $3 million.

They were all good, clean gigs too. They never carried any guns, never hurt a person. They only hit big stores, never a small family business. Kevin figured insurance covered most of their hits. He was proud of that. Never in his life had he done a break-and-enter on someone's house or robbed a bank or shit like that. His jobs were always in the middle of the night. Always quiet. Always no victims. Always at least $20,000.

Kevin smiled. It was like they were cowboys, rooftop cowboys, going from town to town, store to store, and doing their jobs.

"All right, guys. I still want to do this thing. The rain's stopped. It's good. It's dark. We should be in and out easy," announced Kevin. "Everyone in?"

Tyler looked up and gave Kevin one of those don't-ask-such-a-dumb-fucking-question looks and nodded. He had thought this through the past three days. They had a good system going and the last thing they needed was a case of the nerves. He figured continue with the plan, then lay low. Kevin could tell he wasn't worried. When Tyler was really hyped up or on edge, he would start this nervous blinking. It was wild. But right now he was calm and relaxed.

Marc jumped off the bed and reached for the car keys on the desk. He didn't need to answer. "I'm driving motherfuckers."

Yves stayed where he was.

"Yves?"

No answer.

"Yves?" repeated Kevin, louder this time. "Fuck, Yves, what's the problem?"

Still no answer.

What was this? Kevin was losing his temper. One minute Yves is cracking about the pornos, now this. Kevin walked over to the side of the bed and just looked down into Yves's face. He was still smiling, but he shot Marc a dark look before turning back to Kevin. "Well?"

"Ask Marc about the phone call."

"What?"

"Ask Marc about the goddamn phone call."

"What the fuck?" Kevin was getting pissed off. He looked at the TV. Some faggot-ass British pop band was singing on Letterman. Oasis or something like that. It was shit music and when the bands came on, that meant the show was almost over. It was close to 12:30 then. Time to leave.

Kevin liked all the jobs to start around 1 a.m. so there would be a good comfort zone. In total, they took about two hours from the time they parked the car to the time they drove away, but if something went wrong inside, Kevin didn't want to be stuck in the store at 5 a.m., when most early-bird shifts reported to work.

Whatever was going on between Yves and Marc, if things went bad, they could be stuck at the hotel for another hour. That would mess everything up.

"What is this shit?" demanded Kevin.

Marc walked over to the bed where Yves was still lying. "The guy's being a baby. So fucking what? I called my girlfriend while you were in the shower. It's Valentine's Day as of half an hour ago and I promised her I'd call. If you guys had any fucking sense of romance, you'd do the same thing. It's no big deal." Marc shrugged and walked to the door.

Whoa.

Kevin's stomach hurt. He felt ill. He needed a cure for the pain: a sudden urge for a beer or six jumped into his head. This was a really bad sign. Fuck the rain. This was serious.

They had all agreed: No phone calls back to Ottawa from any place they were staying. Since it was a good bet that the phones in their apartments were all tapped, it wasn't that much of a long shot for the police to also get taps on the phones of their girlfriends. If the girls' phones were tapped and if the police were trying to tail them, all it would take is one phone call and the police would have their exact location. If the police had lost them when they left Ottawa, which would explain the get-away at the Shoppers on Sunday, with that one phone call Marc could have put them back on their trail. It wasn't like phone calls were totally banned; they had agreed they could make phone calls from phone booths in some of the towns they stopped in, and as a matter of fact, Kevin and the others had even made some calls from a phone booth in Brantford the other day after they had bought the tools at the Canadian Tire. But the basic rule was simple: no calls from the hotels and no calls from the towns they were actually staying in. Marc had broken the rule.

Kevin really wanted a beer. "You called Terri Anne?"

Marc was at the door. He shrugged again.

"We had a deal . . ." Kevin searched for the right words. He didn't need a fight right now. "If the cops are onto us, that call could have put them onto the hotel. For all we know, the local cops are on their way. If that happens . . ." He trailed off and stared at Marc.

"If. Big fucking if," shot back Marc. He ran his fingers through his hair and did a quick check in the hall mirror. "You guys are paranoid. Yves is a fucking wuss. We have a clean job lined up, we need the money. The police are not onto us. I guarantee you. And even if — *if* — the cops are even close to us, there is no way they'll ID the call, connect it to this shithole and then follow us to the job. There are a fucking hundred stores we could hit within 10 miles of here. There's nothing the cops can do. Let's go."

Kevin looked at the clock. It was quarter to one. If they were going to go they had to go now. Marc was right about one thing. Even in the worst-case scenario, if the cops picked up the call, they would have to get here and tail them. They couldn't possibly know what job they were going to do.

"All right. Here's the plan. We're going now — everyone." Kevin gave Yves a sharp look. "We drive until we know for sure there is no tail. If we even suspect there's police on us, if the heat is there, we call it off. If it's clear, we get to the store, we do the job, quick and clean.

"If the cops are going to get us it'll be back here. That means everyone takes their normal clothes.

"After we score, we dump the clothes and tools and come back to the hotel. Boom, we're clean. We drop off Tyler with the score at the Tim Horton's, come back and clean out the hotel room and we drive back tonight.

"Everyone in?"

Marc just opened the door and walked out. Tyler bent over, wrapped the wiped-down tools in a blanket so they could be taken out to the car.

"Yves? Come on," Kevin said, moving to the door. He turned back. "We need you."

Yves got up off the bed and headed for the door.

Y Y Y

The black pavement was wet, but not icy. The rain had all but tapered out and there was a breeze coming from the south, carrying in the musty scent of Lake Ontario.

It was a mild night, especially compared to what they were used to in Ottawa. When they had left, it was -20°C and there was five feet of snow on the ground. Here in St. Catharines, in balmy southern Ontario, it was a totally different scene. There were traces of snow, sure, but far more grass to be seen. Granted, it was yellow and dead, but Kevin didn't mind. He hated the cold.

Marc's boneheaded phone call reminded him again that it was Valentine's Day. He should do something special for his wife Sylvie when he got back home tomorrow night. If the score went down, he'd buy her something nice. Real nice.

He had even been toying with the idea of moving down to southern Ontario with her. A change of scene would do them good. Maybe, once they let things cool down a bit, the gang could do a big tour, maybe hit nine or ten stores in a two-week period. For once he would save his money, skip the partying, the vacations, the gambling. He could easily round up enough cash to buy a small house and move Sylvie down here.

It would be a good cover for the gang, too. The cops would think they had broken up and all he'd have to do was meet them wherever the jobs were planned.

Kevin was right into the fantasy as he slid into the front seat of the red Sunbird. Yves and Tyler got in the back and Marc pulled the car out of the Howard Johnson parking lot.

They drove around for half an hour, keeping their eyes peeled for anyone following them, but the streets were deserted. They saw a couple of cruisers, but they were parked harmlessly outside a country-and-western bar. There was no sign of a tail.

Marc spoke up first, almost gloating. "Everyone satisfied?"

How could they not be? There were no cars, no people, no tail. St. Catharines had always been a dead town and on this Tuesday night it was an absolute graveyard.

Marc swung the car around and headed for Glenridge Avenue and the Shoppers Drug Mart that was waiting there. It was part of the IGA Plaza, a single-story strip mall with the grocery store, a post office, a hair salon and the Shoppers. American-style suburbia at its worst. There was a huge parking lot in front and even better, loading docks in the back. The dolts who ran the place had been foolish enough to put a garbage Dumpster right against the back wall. All the guys had to do was climb up on that, shimmy up some pipes and they were on the roof.

As they pulled in off Glenridge, Marc steered the car back behind the mall and down a side street. He parked it about a block away, just so there wouldn't be any suspicions raised by a lone car at the Shoppers this time of night. They shut off the engine and listened.

There wasn't even the sound of another car. The place was dead. They got out and strolled down the block, making sure there were no prying eyes in the windows of the homes and apartments. Nothing.

Marc sidled up behind Yves and pinched his ass hard. "Are you happy? We have the run of the place."

Yves only glared at him.

Tyler slipped a crowbar and pick into the waistband of his sweat pants and headed for the Dumpster. The rest of the guys followed suit.

They waited on the ground until Tyler popped his head over the edge of the roof. He had done a look around. Everything was clear. The rest of the guys scrambled up onto the roof, Kevin first and Yves bringing up the rear.

Using tin snips and saws, they were through the roof in no time. As always, they dug through directly above the manager's office, so they could drop down right on top of the safe.

Once they were in, the job was set.

Most businesses set up dozens of complicated and expensive alarm systems in the store and outside the manager's office to stop people from getting in and breaking into the safe. The drug counters got the full treatment too. Drug fiends hungry for a fix were the biggest danger to an isolated Shoppers Drug Mart.

Much to the glee of the gang, no one ever thought to put the high-end alarm systems *inside* the office because they were so confident the outside alarms could never be breached. Of course, they never expected anyone to be coming through the roof. As long as the people in charge of security for these stores suffered such huge brain cramps, the guys figured they could keep on working.

Once down inside the office, Kevin actually started to relax. Yves was making good progress on the safe and Marc was dismantling an alarm that was set up on the inside of the door so they could do a quick check of the rest of the offices to grab anything else they wanted.

Kevin was sitting on the cheap wooden desk and checking out the cramped office. It was pathetic. A ugly wooden coat rack, some of the same goofy Shoppers Drug Mart motivational posters that were on the walls of every office they had ever broken into and a sick-looking plant in the corner. And the relatively new black cube safe that Yves was working on.

Whoever the guy was who had to work in here, Kevin didn't envy him. No windows, shitty job, no life. He took the screwdriver he was holding and dug it into the desktop, taking a huge gouge of wood out it. A little souvenir. His pager started vibrating and he checked the scores in the hockey games. The Canucks had held on to win but the Kings and Sabres were going into overtime, still scoreless.

"How's it coming Yves?"

"Ten more minutes."

The safe was a standard model, a thick metal lining covering its walls of two-inch concrete. The best way to go through them was to use a screwdriver and hammer to pry back the metal near the corner and then start chipping away at the concrete. The corner junction, where two sides met, was the weakest point. After a couple of solid blows, the structure was already starting to crumble.

Yves had opened up a small crack and shone his flashlight inside. "Oh yeah. It's all there. Three money bags, eight bundles of stamps. We should clear fifty easy."

Kevin unfolded a black garbage bag so they could cart away the take.

Then Tyler popped his head through the hole in the roof.

"Uh, Kev."

"What's up Willy?"

"Can you come up here for just a second?" Tyler's eyelids were doing the mambo and there was real urgency in his voice. He was nervous.

"Is there a problem?

"I'm not sure. Just come check this out."

Kevin stood up on the desk and pulled himself up through the hole and onto the roof. Tyler was usually pretty solid so this worried him. He followed Tyler over to the east side of the roof.

"There."

Tyler was pointing to a blue Ford Taurus idling about a block away. There were two men in the car and both had an excellent view of the front of the Shoppers Drug Mart. If Kevin and Tyler had been on street level, it would have been impossible to spot the car behind the gas station's pumps. But from the rooftop, it was impossible to miss.

"Well?"

Kevin scanned the other streets. There were no other cars in sight, but that didn't mean they weren't there.

He left Tyler and walked slowly along the perimeter of the roof looking for another sign that someone else was watching them. When he got back to the spot where Tyler was standing, the car was still there.

"It's the cops right? Right? It's the fucking cops," Tyler spit out, tripping over the syllables.

Kevin took a deep breath. This whole trip had been a complete fuck up.

"I don't know." He walked back to the hole in roof and leaned in. "Pack it up guys, we're leaving."

Yves and Marc had known that something was wrong as soon as Tyler had called for Kevin. If Kevin was telling them to leave, it meant they had to get out fast. Still, Yves couldn't resist . . .

"Another five minutes and we can get the cash at least. We need the score."

Kevin just walked away.

Yves frowned. No answer from Kevin. This was serious. Forget the score.

Yves and Marc left their tools in the manager's office and climbed up through the hole. Kevin and Tyler were already off the roof and halfway down the block towards the car. In less than 30 seconds, Yves and Marc joined them.

Kevin gave a quick briefing.

"Tyler spotted a car. It's been parked behind the gas station for at least 20 minutes. It wasn't there when Tyler made his first check or his second, so it showed up after we got here. Two men inside, can't really tell anything else. We didn't have the binoculars but it looks like a blue Taurus."

He didn't have to say anything else. Undercover cops loved dorky cars like a Taurus. Kevin looked around. Marc was gripping the steering wheel, his knuckles white, while Tyler was staring out the window. Yves spoke first.

"Heat. It's heat. No doubt."

Marc nodded and started up the engine. Kevin was already peeling off his black shirt and groping for his change of clothes. The others followed suit. They threw it all into a garbage bag in the bag seat. They would need to dispose of it. Quickly.

They drove slowly down the block, up out from behind the mall and onto Glenridge Avenue. This was the true test.

All four scanned the streets. Still no sign of movement. Still deserted. And no sign of the blue Taurus.

"Shit."

Kevin screamed and pounded the dash so hard the glove compartment burst open.

"What? What?!"

Marc was swinging his head from side to side, looking for cops. "Fucking Buffalo scored. The Sabres won. Fuck, that's five dimes gone. It was mine."

"Relax, fuck," shot back Marc. "You scared the shit out of me. I nearly drove off the road."

They drove the streets of St. Catharines for a while longer, with Kevin muttering and swearing, with everyone else constantly checking for a tail or the police. Nothing. They headed back to the hotel.

Maybe they were just paranoid.

"We should've finished the job. Maybe. What do you think?" asked Marc as he drove. He was tapping out his nervous energy on the steering wheel.

"Look, if we get stopped and they find the goodies, we're sunk," answered Kevin. "Even if they stop us now, what's the worst that they can prove? That we broke into a drug store and took nothing?" He smiled. "It looks like we're a bunch of amateurs. Even if the charges stick, we'd never get jail time."

They pulled into the hotel parking lot. There were no police there either.

Kevin laughed. Maybe that was the tradeoff. He'd had the five grand plucked from him, but they hadn't gotten pinched. He'd take that deal anytime.

They got out of the car, Yves grabbing the garbage bag of clothes. Kevin walked up beside Marc and slung his arm around his shoulder.

"Well, loverboy, maybe your special phone call was all right. I think we're clean."

"What'd I say? Trust me." Marc flipped his hair out of his eyes and fumbled in his pocket for the keys to the hotel room. Yves was already making plans to watch the pornos.

"Think they got any good call girls in this town?" he cracked.

Then they saw the blue Taurus.

It was parked in the spot right in front of the hotel manager's office.

Kevin and Tyler froze.

"What? Let's go get some erotic nights. Come on," urged Yves.

Tyler pointed at the car.

"What?"

"That's the one we saw from the roof. They're here."

"Fuck. Yves, dump the bag. Quick."

Yves ran behind the hotel, threw the bag in an emergency stairwell and ran back to the car. That was it. Screw the clothes and shit they had in the hotel room. They were gone. Back to Ottawa. Forget this night. Forget this whole trip. They'd figure out another way to get the money.

Marc got back behind the wheel of the Sunbird. The car didn't start. He looked at Kevin who was staring at the Taurus. He quickly tried again, the Sunbird coughed, the engine turned over, and Marc backed out of the parking space.

That's when they saw the marked police cars.

The whole fucking armada of them.

A dozen cruisers came up over the hill into the hotel parking lot. Each one had their lights blazing, the entire night sky was lit. But it was eerily quiet. The cops hadn't turned their sirens on. There was no need to.

The hotel parking lot was a dead end. They were stuck out in the suburbs of St. Catharines. There was no place to go. There was no point in even trying.

"Fuck me," Kevin whispered as he stared at the lights.

He winced.

After five years on the job and more than $6 million in sweet rewards, it was all coming to a screeching halt.

They were going down.

Chapter TWO

February 22, 1994
Ottawa, Ontario

Yves Belanger stumbled into the Pronto convenience store and brushed the snow off of his gray Polo jacket. Damn it was cold.

He blew a deep breath into his hands to try and warm them up. He should have worn some gloves, but figured it was only two blocks from his apartment to the store, so why bother. It was February in Ottawa and it was snowing. Yves shook his head, sending snow and water spraying out of his tight-curled hair. He should have bothered.

It was just after 11 in the morning and up until 15 minutes ago, Yves had been dead asleep. He and the guys had gone out last night, first to On Tap in the Market and then across the river to the Auzone Club in Hull. With Ontario bars closing at 1 a.m., they usually ended up in Hull where drinks were served until 3 a.m. for everyone and sometimes right up until 5 a.m. if you were a good-enough customer. Naturally, Yves and the rest of the guys were good-enough customers.

From what Yves remembered, it was a damn fine time. He must have dropped $800, what with all the food and drinks he had bought. Hell, he must have dropped $200 dollars alone on . . . Laurel? Was that her name? Yves couldn't think. He shook his head in an attempt to clear the fog of his hangover. It wasn't working. He sighed.

It was the one mistake from last night. The girl was still back at his apartment. When he had left this morning, she was in the bathroom brushing her teeth. He ran. It was the only thing he could do. Fuck. The thought of kissing her again made him ill.

Yeah. She was definitely a mistake.

Laurel was typical Hull trash: peroxide-blond hair, heavy make-up and a strong liver. As soon as she saw the kind of money Yves was tossing around, she was all over him. He should have known better than to take her home. Did they even use a condom? Yves tried to think. He couldn't remember. His fucking memory was failing like a dying car battery on a dark road. And worse, he couldn't even remember if the sex was good. That was bad. He must have drunk a barrel of Canadian Club last night.

Yves groaned again. His head pounded. He tried to put last night out of his mind. He needed more sleep, but Kevin had called him, really upset. Go get the newspaper, he had insisted. There's some bad news. Yves had wanted to ask him more, but they had a simple rule: never discuss business on the phone.

Yves looked around the Pronto, but before grabbing a paper, he walked back to the cooler to grab a bottle of Five Alive. Yves didn't care how bad the news was. He was hungover and needed some juice. After cracking open the bottle, he headed for the stack of papers. What could have wired up Kevin so badly?

He didn't have to wait long to find out. There it was, splashed all over the front page of the *Ottawa Citizen*. As of today, February 22, 1994, the taxes on cigarettes were cut. Not just cut. Fucking slashed. Big time.

The Province of Ontario had announced, in an effort to combat the increased cigarette smuggling on Native reserves along the American border, they were cutting the price of smokes in half. That meant a carton of cigarettes which sold for $41 last week would go for just $23. This was bad for business.

Yves stared down at the front page of the *Citizen*. No wonder Kevin was so upset. This was really bad for business.

"Fucking government."

Yves spat on the photo of the politician staring up from the front of the paper. Bastard was grinning like Miss America after making the cigarette announcement. Good for him, bad for the little guys. Trying to make an honest hard-working dollar or three.

"Bureaucratic prick." Yves spat again.

When he looked up, the store clerk was looking nervously at him.

"Don't sweat it man. I'm buying it, I'm buying it."

Asshole. Yves paid for the drink and the paper and headed back out into the freezing February air. The cold wind was beating into his face and snow was stinging his eyes.

Yes. There was no doubt about it.

This was starting out to be a real shitty day.

Y Y Y

Three hours later, Yves was sitting alone at a table for four at the Lone Star Cafe in the west end of Ottawa. The other guys — Kevin, Marc and Tyler — were due to arrive in about 15 minutes. Yves had come early, wanting to think a bit before the meeting.

He took a swig of Molson Dry. It had almost hurt to order the beer, but it was the only cure for a hangover. He took another gulp. It was working.

By the time Yves had gotten back to his apartment with the paper, the girl was gone. So was a 26er of rye he kept in his fridge. And some CDs. Both Pearl Jam discs. The day just got worse. Maybe the other guys knew who she was. Then Yves could track her down and teach her a lesson.

At least he had found a used condom beside the bed. It was still damp, so it must have been from last night. That was very good. Who knew what the skank was carrying.

He had read the article on the cigarette cuts twice before calling Kevin back. Kevin was calm by then and had already made calls to the other guys to set up the meeting at the Lone Star. That was one thing Yves respected about him. No matter what the situation, Kevin was good at taking control, and everybody seemed to listen to him.

Yves took another swig of beer, finishing the bottle. He waved at the waitress for another and began digging into the free bowl of chips and salsa.

He could see why Kevin had panicked. The cigarette-tax cut was really going to hurt the gang. No question.

For the past two years, the guys had been doing lucrative business in the cigarette trade. Yves figured he'd been pulling in at least $6,000 a month doing the work. And all four of the guys were making about the same thing. It was the sweetest deal they'd ever had. And they could have kept it up for years if it wasn't for the smuggling.

The government had cut the taxes to stop the smuggling, which was starting to cause real havoc along the U.S.-Canada border. The guys were nowhere near that part of the business. Not at all.

The smuggling end was controlled by the Mohawks down at the Akwesasne Reserve. The Mohawks had land straddling the American border so they bought Canadian cigarettes in the U.S. by the truckload and moved them into Canada without having to pass any border controls.

Because cigarettes shipped to the United States didn't have any of the Canadian taxes on them, they sold for about $12 U.S. a carton. The Mohawks would run the cartons into Montreal, Ottawa and Toronto and sell the cartons for between $25 or $30 Canadian each. According to the newspaper article, smugglers were moving as many as 10,000 cartons a day across the border. There were stories of guys with fleets of boats and trucks, all used to move the hot smokes.

It was quick, easy money. You never saw so many Indians driving BMWs.

No way the guys could touch that market. And, really, they didn't want any part of it. It was too competitive and too hot. Police had been trying to bust up the smuggling rings for the past two years and there were always arrests being made.

No, the guys made their money because the cigarette prices were so high, they were a hot item to steal. And stealing was what the crew did best.

Yves looked up. The waitress had finally arrived with his second beer. No, he didn't want a menu yet. He turned in his chair, and scanned the doorway, but there was still no sign of the guys.

When it came to cigarettes, the gang had two different types of jobs.

The first was Yves's favourite. Using a three-man crew inside and a driver outside, the guys would hit a convenience store — a Mac's Milk, a Becker's, whatever was begging to be relieved of their inventory.

Those places were so cheap, they usually only had one clerk working the store at any given time. That meant it was a joke job for the gang.

Two guys would go in as decoys, buy some Doritos or an Oh Henry bar and go up to the counter. Then they'd start buying scratch-and-win lottery tickets from the clerk, two or three at a time and scratch them right there at the counter.

While they were doing this the third guy, and it was usually Yves because he was the best back-room guy among them, would come in and go to the back of the store.

With the guys going crazy on the scratch-and-wins — "No, no, fucking shit. I lost again," Marc would play it up real good — the clerk had to stay at the counter. Store policy was that you couldn't leave people there at the cash with access to the tickets. The clerk never really worried about the third guy who came in. When the stores paid them $6 an hour and made them wear goofy uniforms, the clerks usually weren't too concerned about catching shoplifters. With the clerk occupied, the target was the cases of cigarettes stacked in the back room.

Nine times out of ten the door between the store and the back room was locked or there was a buzzer that went off when it was opened to warn the clerk. That was fine. Yves never went through the door.

Almost every convenience store had the same layout, with the cooler for juice and milk up against the back wall. The coolers had two-way access so they could be stocked from back room without blocking the aisles.

It was a smart design in that sense. But the designers hadn't anticipated convenience-store opportunists like Yves.

While the two guys acting as decoys were scratching lottery tickets at the front counter, Yves would slide open the door to the milk fridge. As quiet as possible, he would push aside the bags of milk and lift out the white racks they were kept on. Then, with a quick check over his shoulder to make sure no one was watching, he would squirm into the cooler. All he had to do then was go through the second cooler door and he was in the back room. He always had a couple of garbage bags down his pants so he could cart away the goods.

Once Yves got into the back room, he had all the time in the world. The clerk either forgot about him or got confused and figured Yves had left the store without him noticing. To make the set up even sweeter, there was always a camera focused on the front counter with a tape running. With the frequency with which these stores were held up, management liked to have a tape of the robbery to give to police. And of course, there was a television hooked up to the monitor in the back room so the clerk could watch the floor if he went to get supplies.

So while Yves was loading up the garbage bags with cartons of cigarettes, he could watch the monitor to make sure the clerk was still at the counter. If he started for the back, Yves would just head out the back door, which was never alarmed because that was the only way to take the garbage out or for the clerk to go out and have a smoke himself. Sweet.

Yves could usually pack about 40 or 50 cartons in each bag, taking about 250 or 300 for the score. Once he was done, he would leave by the back door and meet the driver who was waiting outside with the car running. Because Yves would always leave the back room neat and try to replace the racks and milk in the fridge, it meant the store rarely noticed the crime. At least not until an inventory count came up about 200 cartons short. By then it was too late to connect it to anyone and the owners usually blamed one of the hapless employees.

Once Yves was in car, the driver would pull up in front of the store just long enough for the guys playing scratch-and-win to catch a glimpse of the car, so they'd know the job was done.

The guys playing the lottery would keep at it for another 10 minutes or so, wait until more customers came in so the clerk wouldn't have time to think, and then take off.

The score always took less than half an hour, and considering they could sell the cartons on the black market for $27 a pop, usually netted between $5,000 and $8,000. It was easy money. And they had done it so often, sometimes it seemed they had hit every convenience store within a 200-mile radius of Ottawa. Twice.

Yves was smiling as he thought about those jobs. Learn one skill well, his school teachers told him, it's the best way to get ahead. Well he was a goddamn genius, and like he'd been promised, he was ahead by a country mile. The beer was starting to taste real good.

He loved the cigarette work. He could never understand why idiots would do something like rob a bank. The take for a bank job was about the same $3,000 to $4,000 but you had all those witnesses, alarms went off immediately and you usually needed to carry a weapon. He had a friend who had done a bank job and the teller had stuck a goddamn dye bomb in his bag. He had run two blocks, and then boom! — he and the money were covered in red ink. Yves had never laughed so hard the next day when his buddy showed up at his door, still covered with the stuff, even though he had nearly scrubbed his skin off. And of course, police responded like 60 to the armed robberies, they were so quick, it wasn't even funny. It was just stupid to try one. The jobs were too risky and you faced serious jail time if you got caught. The convenience-store jobs were a breeze in comparison and netted the same cash. Thieves weren't the brightest guys, Yves noted, making an exception for himself and the boys.

The gang's second cigarette score was a bit more risky but still a good gig and nowhere near as dangerous as a bank job. It was only a three-man job, so the guys would rotate on who would stay home.

First the guys would locate a big drug store in a quiet part of town. One of the crew, usually Yves or Kevin, would be the inside man and go into the store about an hour before closing, while the store was still pretty busy. The big drug stores always had lots of little rooms in the back — closets where they kept mops, store rooms, bathrooms. It was like a maze.

All the guy had to do was sneak into the back rooms, find a good hiding place and wait. It was cramped and stressful, but after two or three hours, once the employees had left and the store shut down, the inside man was in the clear.

Using a cell phone, he'd call the two other guys, who would pull up behind the store. The inside man would fill four garbage bags full of cigarette cartons and stack them beside the back door. Then he'd sit and wait until he heard the signal — usually three short bursts of the car horn.

After that, he'd fling open the back door, which meant setting off the alarms, but that wasn't a problem. The response time of police was two minutes at best, considering the alarm company had to put the call into the police dispatcher, who would then signal the closest cruiser.

Two minutes was an eternity. The guys were gone in 20 seconds.

The inside man would hand off two of the garbage bags to one of the other guys who was stationed at the door. The two would then head for the car, which was running and pointed out onto the street with the trunk open. All four bags in the trunk, the guys into the back seat and the driver would be gone.

It was a simple, age-old gig. Break-outs or peekaboos, where guys broke out of stores with the goods instead of breaking in, had been around for years. But the gang had it down perfect. With three men working a job, there was almost no risk of getting caught in the act. The worst thing that could happen is that one of the guys would be caught in the back room. It was embarrassing, but if you told them you were just looking for the bathroom, what could they do? Charge you with trespassing?

And money-wise, it was superb. They always pulled in at least $12,000 a gig. But considering the inside guy had to waste three hours in a fucking broom closet with the risk of being caught inside by a probing employee, the easier, but less profitable, convenience-store jobs were the gang's favourite.

And it was never a problem to get rid of the smokes.

Kevin and Yves had hooked up with a guy in Gatineau, John Steinbachs, who ran a legitimate business supplying convenience stores with chips, gum, chocolate bars — and cigarettes.

Steinbachs was the kind of guy with a different money-making scheme every week, always looking for an edge. One time he had even gone up to the Yukon in hopes of starting up a bottled water company called Yukon Pure. Water wasn't the problem — there was a lot of good water — it was the cold, the goddamn cold, Steinbachs would explain. Whine would have been a better word.

He was the kind of guy who didn't mind bending the rules, especially when it meant he could get cartons for $10 cheaper than what the tobacco companies sold them at. He was making a huge profit reselling the gang's hot cigarettes and none of the convenience stores knew the difference. Hell, Yves, Marc, Tyler and Kevin figured some of the stores were actually buying their own cigarettes back. This made Yves happy as hell when he thought about it.

With more than 100 stores on his route, John could move 500 cartons a week, as long as they were popular brands like du Maurier and Player's. It was a virtually perfect scam. Maximum money, minimum risk.

Yves groaned. But it was all in jeopardy now.

With the government tax cut, the price of a carton was a measly $23 bucks. That meant a top price on the street of $13 a carton, more likely $10 or $11.

Yves was no mathematician, but you didn't have to be to figure the numbers out. The gang was screwed. Their income was going to drop in half. Yves finished his second beer and brought the bottle down on the table hard. A little too hard. A group of three wanna-be cowboys sitting at the next table were staring at him.

Yves grinned. "Suck me."

One the guys, decked out in a jean shirt and brown leather cowboy boots, spun around. He was a beefy guy, balding and with a huge gut. He glowered at Yves and began to get out of his chair. One of his sidekicks, a thin-looking hick with a kerchief around his neck and scraggly sideburns, moved to get up as well.

Yves thought he was going to have some fun.

Just as the fat cowboy started to say something, he stopped. He sheepishly dropped back into his chair, lowered his eyes and returned to his half-finished meal.

What the?

Yves turned around.

Behind him stood Kevin, Tyler and Marc, all looking big and mean. Reinforcements had arrived. No wonder the guy lost his confidence.

Fuck that fat-ass anyway.

There were business matters on the agenda.

Y Y Y

"Holy shit, Yves," snapped Marc as he pointed to the empty Molson Dry bottle. "Drinking again? You're a fucking animal."

Marc sat down next to Yves and gave him an elbow to the ribs. Then he caught the eye of the waitress. Not half bad, Marc thought. He gave her a wink and promised himself he would get her number before he left the restaurant.

"Let's have a round then, shall we boys?" he announced.

Kevin and Tyler sat down, but Tyler was still looking at the cowboys.

"What was that, Yves?"

"It was nothing. I just told him to suck me off."

"Oh that's good," said Kevin as he grabbed a menu from the waitress. "This is a nice family restaurant and you're looking to go at it with a bunch of fucking rednecks. You're a gentleman, Yves."

They ordered the beer and some fajitas. Marc started into Yves right away.

"That was some sweetie you took home last night, eh Yves?"

"Fuck you, Marc."

"She looked so pure and innocent. Virgin-like. You must have been her first lover."

"Fuck you, Marc."

"But I'm sure she had a great personality, eh? Probably the kind of girl you could marry."

Yves was pissed. Fucking Marc. There was no way he could bring up the CDs and rye that whore had snatched without losing total face. He would look like an oaf.

Kevin leaned in and began to speak.

"Okay, look. Yves has some pretty bad taste in women when he's been drinking. We've known it for a long time. But we need to talk. Seriously."

Yves didn't say anything.

"Okay," Kevin continued. "I talked to Steinbachs today. First off, he thinks we're a bunch of idiots. Hasn't anyone been watching the news?"

He looked around the table. The six glassy, hangover eyes staring back at him pretty much answered that one.

"This cigarette-tax cut thing was in the pipes for months. I think everyone knew it was coming but us.

"Second, Steinbachs says he can still handle our cigarettes, but no fucking surprise, at a way cut rate. He says no more than $10 a carton. It's peanuts, but he says it's the best he can do. The fucker."

The waitress came with a pitcher of beer and four rye and cokes. They sat in silence, thinking about what Kevin had just said. At $10 a carton, that meant the scores would be way down. It would mean only $2,500 or so for a convenience-store job — less than $700 each, or $5,000 for the drug stores, which they all hated doing.

This was not a good scene.

The guys had been working the cigarette angle for the past two and a half years. It was their best source of income and, really, it was the gig that had made the gang what they were.

Sure, before the cigarette jobs started in 1992, they had worked together for about a year, but it was real casual. A job here, a job there, nothing set in stone. It was the usual grab bag of crime. A lot of smash-and-grabs, where they drove by a stereo store in the middle of the night, smashed the window, grabbed the inventory and were gone in two minutes. Some peekaboos at sports stores, some jobs at offices. Nothing fancy. Certainly no $6,000 a month.

Y Y Y

The pieces started to fall in place during the summer of 1990.

Kevin was just 22 at the time and had been working since he was 13. It was always little stuff, break-ins at convenience stores, smash-grabs at electronics stores, maybe hiding in a ski shop overnight and running out with some jackets. Little bullshit jobs that scored $300 or $400 at most. He was doing five or six jobs a month, tops. It was enough to help pay the rent but little else. He needed more money, he had been living on his own or with Sylvie since he was 17, after his mom died. At first he had thought about going for some honest work, but he had long ago given up his job at the Macdonald-Cartier International Airport, where he had worked part time as a baggage handler, and committed himself to earning money in the shadows. Lately though, he was getting pissed because the guys he was working with were screwing him around. For a load of Gore-Tex jackets that should have netted $5,000, Kevin would only get a $500 cut. He needed new partners.

That summer he had met Tyler at a party. The two ended up drinking together all night, doing JD shooters and drinking Blue. Tyler had worked before, little break-and-enters for kicks and what not, but that summer he was pumping gas, a shitty minimum-wage job with a boss who thought that for $5.25 an hour you were his fucking slave. Tyler had also been a pretty earnest kid, serious about school and wild about hockey. But even the thrill of being the star goalie on his school's hockey team paled in comparison to the full-scale adrenaline explosion of a little bit of illegal activity.

As they drank, they exchanged stories, romanticizing past breakins and scores. As the Jack Daniels disappeared, Tyler became more animated, his reserve going out the window. Right around dawn, when the beer was gone and there was only a couple of shots left in the bottle of Jack, Kevin took a dumb risk.

After hearing Tyler whine about how much he hated his job for the past hour, Kevin came up with a suggestion.

"Let's do a job there, you and me," he proposed.

Kevin was bagged or else he would have never asked. He knew enough not to talk about work, especially with some guy he barely knew. This guy could talk, his dad could be a cop. Hell, Kevin could have even hit the family business in one of his earlier jobs.

But Kevin got lucky.

"What kind of job?" was Tyler's only answer.

Kevin quickly peppered him with questions. When does the gas station have the most money in its till? Does the owner go to the bank every night? Does he keep the day's receipts in a safe or in a drawer? What kind of locks were on the door?

Tyler was getting excited.

By the time the last of the Jack was gone, the sun had risen and the two had come up with a plan to break into Tyler's gas station the next Friday night. They figured they could walk with close to $1,000 in cash, a great score. Police always immediately suspected an inside job, but Tyler was confident he could play dumb and fool the cops *and* the owner if he was questioned.

The next Friday night they pulled the job, with Kevin going in and Tyler standing watch outside. It went smooth and easy.

The next day, Tyler played the straight man. The boss didn't hit him too hard with questions. It was only $1,000. Insurance covered the whole hit. But the day at work was hell. It must have been 35°C.

For the rest of the summer, the two did small jobs together. The set up was always the same. Tyler was the outside man and Kevin did the inside work. Kevin also kept 60 per cent of each score because the inside man did the more difficult work. Tyler was fine with the arrangement. He did little to nothing on each hit, just kept a lookout, was suspicious of nearby activity, and if the hit was successful, and they almost always were, he'd done a good job.

It was a great team. Kevin found someone he liked and could trust to work with. Tyler had found a good source of income and loved the excitement. He also liked Kevin's sense of morals.

While other guys Kevin knew were doing break-and-enters at family homes, stealing VCRs, TVs and jewellery, Kevin stuck to businesses.

"That's for sleazebags, hitting people at home," Kevin explained to Tyler one night over beers. "The businesses have insurance. We can do these things with a clean conscience, trust me. Nobody gets hurt."

After the summer was over, Tyler, who was still just 19, headed to Woodroffe High School to finish Grade 13. He had started out his high school at Laurentien, where he had been the goalie on the hockey team, but transferred to Woodroffe because it was a semester school and he just needed a half-year to finish.

By chance, Yves Belanger and Marc Flamini, both 16, were going into Grade 10 that year at the same high school. The two were pretty close friends, having gone to public school together, and the year before they had dated girls who were best friends. Of course, those relationships ended when Marc and Yves tried to convince the girls that they should swap partners for a night. Not only did they refuse, they left. But a solid friendship was set in cement.

They hung out a lot, skipping classes and spending their days looking for girls or figuring out new ways to boost things from the neighbourhood mall. Even then, Marc was into his clothes, either buying or shoplifting the finest items the Carlingwood Mall had to offer. When they were at school, the two got in trouble, getting rung up for missed classes and mouthing off to the teachers.

Normally Tyler would have never known either of them, what with three years' difference between them. But over the summer, Yves had started up a little business. A little steroid business. And one of Tyler's friends was among his best customers.

Yves had been working since he was 10 years old. He had been in every type of business — stealing cars, break-and-enters, drugs, now the steroids. He also had a nose for who else was working. Over the summer, he had heard that Tyler was doing jobs and had a good connection. Yves wanted to know what was up and maybe even get Tyler in on a couple of jobs with him.

One night in October, when a bunch of guys were at Tyler's house in Nepean, Yves showed up to deliver a batch of Anadrol 50. After collecting his money, Yves sat down and had a beer. Soon he was involved in an intense game of poker, quickly doubling his steroid money. Late into the night, after Yves had ordered and paid for a round of pizzas to help soothe any hurt feelings, he excused himself from the game and asked Tyler if they could talk outside. In private.

"I hear you're in the business."

Tyler played dumb.

"Look, I just have a proposal. You'll like working with me. Easy money. All the time. No risks."

Tyler still wouldn't admit to anything. But Yves persisted.

"Look, I know you've doing jobs with that Grandmaison guy. It's all over the place. I need someone who's strong and solid. I want you in."

Yves's words made Tyler nervous. He wasn't a criminal, he just had a hobby, a fetish of sorts, and now it seemed like all his dirty laundry was blowing in the wind for all the world to see. He assumed no one had known about Kevin's and his work. He didn't tell anyone. And he thought Kevin was keeping quiet too. Maybe the kid was bluffing but it pissed him off.

"Look," Tyler finally answered, trying to sound unshaken. "I don't want to talk about anything here. This is my mom's house. I'll talk to you tomorrow at school. All right?"

Yves smiled. His foot was in the door.

As soon as everyone had left, Tyler called Kevin.

How did Yves know?

Kevin had no idea. He had never even heard of this Yves guy. But Kevin did have a plan. He would come with Tyler for a meeting with Yves. They would meet at a public place, say Baxter's Restaurant on Merivale on Saturday night. Kevin would check him out. If he was solid, well, maybe they could work something out together. If he wasn't . . .

"Don't worry, Tyler. We won't let some shitface 16-year-old fuck with us. If something's up, I'll handle it."

The next day at school, Yves came up to Tyler in the cafeteria. Tyler gave him the invitation. Done deal. Saturday night was on. Yves, always cautious, didn't warn Tyler that he would bring a friend, Marc, just as some insurance. Yves wasn't going to let himself be set up.

When Yves and Marc got to Baxter's, Kevin and Tyler were already there. No one seemed surprised to see Marc. Yves put his cards on the table right away.

He and Marc had been working with a friend's brother the past couple of months. Easy jobs, break-and-enters and what not. But the guy was stupid, and he took 60 per cent of the cut, Marc and Yves only 20 per cent each. Now they wanted something bigger with more money. The plan they wanted Tyler in on was for a bingo hall in the west end. Lots of cash receipts kept in the filing cabinet each night. They wanted a driver who also acted as a lookout, and two guys inside.

This is where Tyler fit into the equation.

It was a good proposal and Kevin and Tyler listened. Everyone seemed solid and everyone got along. That was good. But more important, Kevin immediately recognized how rare the group was.

One of the things that had initially attracted him to Tyler was how clean-cut the guy was. He wore his blond hair in an athlete's buzz cut, wore preppy Club Monaco clothes and could be as polite as a funeral director. Tyler could walk into any store, scope it out and never raise an eyebrow.

What Kevin had learned in his years working was that there were always dozens of dope heads who were eager to work, the kind of guys you wouldn't want to be seen walking down the street with. These guys, with their bad-ass attitudes, long hair and tattoos, drew heat and raised suspicion. They could also be stupid. They would brag about their jobs to anyone who would listen. Working with them was suicide.

But the four guys around the table that night at Baxter's could have stepped out of a Gap catalogue. They were all clean and looked trustworthy. And after a couple of hours of conversation, it was easy to tell each had a head for the game. They were smart enough to know when to talk, when not to. It was a dream crew.

As they left the bar, with Marc and Yves talking about the Porches they'd be driving this time next year, the four agreed to do a test job together. The next night they would hit the bingo job that Yves had proposed.

They met at Kevin's place just after midnight. Everyone was on time. No one had been drinking or smoking weed. They all wore loose dark clothes and had brought along their own pair of gloves. Kevin was impressed.

The bingo was in an old warehouse and as far the guys knew, there no alarms whatsoever. It looked simple. And it was.

They drove over in Kevin's blue Mustang. Tyler stayed behind the wheel while Marc, Kevin and Yves went inside through the back door. The locks were cheap, the manager's office easy to find and the cashiers' tills were in a desk drawer with a lock a two-year-old could have broken.

In less than five minutes, without breaking a sweat, they were back on the road with $1,400 to split among them.

It was the start of a beautiful relationship. After that first night, they ended up doing a couple of jobs a month together. It wasn't an exclusive arrangement. Tyler and Kevin did jobs on the side and Yves seemed to have his finger in a new scheme every week.

It was one of these schemes that led to the promised land of cigarettes. A friend of Yves told him his brother was looking for guys to do some daylight jobs with him. All Yves would have to do is stand at the cash register and keep the clerk occupied for five minutes. In return, Yves would get $100. It seemed too easy to be true.

One night while at On Tap playing pool, Yves described the jobs to Kevin. They were easy and the guy Yves was working with was another bonehead. He would only grab 15 or 20 cartons and then sell them to his friends. He only hit one or two stores a month. Yves figured that if they had the crew working and a way to distribute the cigarettes, it could mean a windfall.

Kevin loved the idea. A couple of months back, he had met Steinbachs, the distribution guy. A friend had done a gas station and taken a case of smokes and Steinbachs was the fence. Kevin told Yves he could probably move a high volume of smokes without too much trouble. They came up with the plan involving all four guys.

The day they pulled their first one, it was amazing. All that money in so little time. After a couple of months doing the convenience-store jobs, they came up with the plan for breaking out of the drug stores. It was money time.

Y Y Y

It *was* money time.

Kevin downed his rye and then took a sip of his beer. It was time to decide what to do about the tax cut.

"Well?"

Yves started. "That's a huge cut. I don't know man, but I'm not going to be wiggling my ass into back rooms for $700. We need a different gig."

Marc nodded. There was no doubt in his mind. They needed to make serious money. He was just getting by now, and that was with sharing a two-bedroom apartment with Tyler. He wanted to move out on his own, and it would take some serious finances to set up his place the way he wanted it. The reduced cigarette scores just wouldn't cut it.

"Look, it was a good run, but now it's over. We can still do the jobs, sure. But we'd have to do twice as many to get the same money. And seriously, I got nothing in the bank. I'm barely surviving on what I get right now."

Tyler was quiet.

He figured what the hell. It was still good money. Who else could make $700 in half an hour? Some people didn't even make that in a week. But he knew he didn't need the money as much as the others. Kevin and Yves gambled. Big time. Hockey, baseball, football, whatever. He went to Las Vegas last year with Kevin and the guy dropped $25,000 on the weekend. That was serious coin. Marc lost some to the betting, but he spent most of his take on travelling and clothes. Every time you looked, the guy had a new suit, a new woman on his arm and a plane ticket to Bermuda, Jamaica or some other ocean paradise.

"I'm with you guys, but we don't need to do anything stupid," Tyler said, speaking softly. "I think we still have a good racket here. Even if we make half of what we do now, I'm still making more money than anyone else I know." Tyler paused. Then . . . "But whatever. I'm in."

Kevin nodded. He was glad the guys were ready to move on. He certainly wasn't going to risk his ass for shit money. The guys were ready for a change. And he had a plan.

"I think we might have something else lined up anyway. It's safe and easy. Trust me."

Marc, Yves and Tyler looked at Kevin. The waitress came with food, so they had to wait until she was done unloading the plates and the food.

Yves broke the silence.

"What the hell are you talking about, Kevin?"

Kevin smiled.

"Boys. Cam Woloski wants to have dinner with us."

Chapter THREE

March 1994
Ottawa, Ontario

The four of them sat in the car and waited, their breath exploding into mist as it hit the frigid air. No one talked.

They all just stared at the little white bungalow with the lights that seemed to blaze from every window. A giant German Shepherd was chained in the back yard and the guys could see its eyes glowing green against the dark night sky as the animal stared at the car.

"Well. Should we go in?"

It was Yves, who was sitting in the back seat of Marc's Z-24 along with Tyler. Kevin, sitting in the passenger seat, checked the clock on the dash.

"It's only 8:15. He told us not to show up before 8:30. I don't want to piss him off."

Yves nodded. No one wanted to piss off Cam Woloski.

They had been at Kevin's apartment, passing the time before their appointment and beating back a 40 of rye to calm their nerves. They were so worried about being late they had left half an hour early. Now they were sitting in Marc's car, freezing their asses off and nervous as hell. That rye hadn't done much good.

Kevin's stomach was hurting. It was like meeting the pope.

"Turn up the heater, man. It's cold." It was Yves again, complaining.

An icy March wind was howling outside the car, and monstrous white snow banks still towered on either side of the street outside of Woloski's house. Marc let out a smile and nudged the heat control a few degrees colder. Yves had spilled a glass of CC on his blue Hugo Boss blazer while they were at Kevin's place and now he stunk of alcohol. What would Woloski think? Let Yves freeze his nuts off in the back seat, the careless fucker. Marc hesitated, thought of the dry-cleaning bill, and then pushed the control to maximum, letting cold air blast into the car.

"I don't know what's going on, Yves. I think the thing's broken." Marc smiled again and leaned in so he could check out his hair in the rear view mirror. Even if he did stink like rye, he looked hot. They were all decked out for the big meeting.

Woloski had put a call in to Kevin in January, wanting to know if his gang was willing to do some work with him. It was a stunning offer and Kevin was flattered. More than flattered. Woloski was as big as they came in Ottawa. As far as the stories went — and that was all there was with Woloski, stories — the guy had his finger in every major score in the city. Drugs, prostitution, car theft, counterfeit money — you name it, Woloski was there.

He was a short guy, with salt-and-pepper hair and weathered skin that bore the lines of too many nights of hard living. He was in his early 40s, but if you passed him on the street, you would guess he was in his 60s. The eeriest thing about him was his teeth, which he had had capped with gold when he was just a hood working the streets of Montreal in the 1970s. That gold had become dark and grimy from years of smoking and drinking. Now when he smiled it was like looking into the ugly black maw of death.

The cops were always trying to take him down. The major crime unit of the Ottawa police had spent more than $1 million on a six-month sting operation in 1989 that was supposed to net Woloski and put him behind bars for life. But "Project Hammerhead" had turned to shambles after some of Woloski's goons shoved a gun in the face of an undercover cop who didn't quite get the "under" part of cover. The cop lost his cool and his back-up lost his nerve and called for help. Within seconds, a half-dozen cruisers had blocked the street off. The goons dropped their gun and the police swarmed in to make the arrests. In total, they got three men, all minor players, on drug and weapons charges. No one would roll over on Woloski. Project Hammerhead was blown.

That fiasco had only made Woloski stronger and left the budget-minded police force too timid to spend the kind of money that it would take to bring him down. They continued making petty arrests, taking out part of Woloski's ring, but the ringleader never fell.

He had been at the top of the city's action for more than a decade and had stayed there with two simple policies: be smart and be ruthless. He treated everyone who worked for him well, paid good money for jobs, and treated loyal workers with respect. But if someone working for him got out of line . . .

The best story Kevin and the guys had ever heard about Woloski involved a two-timing crook named Drew Edwards.

Edwards, a sinister-looking man with a bad limp courtesy of an ancient bullet, had been running hash for Woloski for about two years. While doing time in the pen for some armed robberies in the Guelph area, Edwards had met one of Woloski's boys, who had set him up with work when Edwards got parole. It was a simple deal. Edwards would drive down to New Brunswick to meet one of the boats from Africa. He would pick up the package, usually 100 kilograms of hash packed tight into two heavy suitcases. Edwards would then drive the drugs, which had a street value of $1 million, back up to Ottawa.

Edwards made the run once a month and got paid $10,000 cash for his work. It was the kind of money hustlers could only dream of. But one winter a couple of years back, Edwards made a fatal mistake. He fell in love.

He had hooked up with Shenendoah, a 17-year-old prostitute working the streets of Hintonburgh for Woloski. The two had come up with a two-bit scheme to start a new life together: hijack one of the hash runs and head to Florida.

So one night, instead of taking the hash to Woloski for inspection, Edwards headed for a trailer park in Richmond, a sleepy town just outside of Ottawa. He was going to lay low there for a couple of days, put some time between when he disappeared and when Shenendoah did.

According to rumour, Woloski lost it. He had picked Edwards out of the gutter and gave him a job, first as a street dealer then doing the drug run. He trusted Edwards. Edwards had betrayed him. Woloski wanted revenge.

And he found it quickly.

Unfortunately for the young couple, Shenendoah had a bit of a crack habit. An even worse habit was she tended to talk when high. Talk a lot.

Police found Shenendoah's naked body stuffed into a garbage bag behind a bar in Ottawa's east-end. A couple of weeks later, when the snow began to melt, police began finding parts of a man's body in the snow banks alongside the highway heading out of Richmond. They never found the whole body or could never identify the man. But Edwards was never seen or heard from again. And both murders remain unsolved.

That was the rumour, anyway.

But Kevin, like most of the other working guys in the city, didn't find it that hard to believe. And now they were going to have dinner with Woloski.

When he had called in January with the offer to work with him, Kevin had turned Woloski down — very politely. They were making good money, so why get into something they couldn't handle? But when the cigarette scam went sour, Kevin got a little bit desperate. He called a friend he knew who worked for Woloski and told him the guys wanted to talk to Woloski. Kevin's phone rang 15 minutes before he was going to leave for the February afternoon meeting at the Lone Star.

Woloski wanted to have dinner.

Kevin leaned against the car door and looked at the house again. Pangs of doubt gnawed at his stomach. What had he gotten them into?

"Okay guys, come on. It's 8:30," said Marc, breaking the silence. Everybody took a deep breath.

They were going in.

Y Y Y

For a man who made a couple of million a year, Woloski's house looked like shit. Cracked walls, a green shag rug and furniture that the Salvation Army wouldn't take. He had some crappy posters on the wall that were squeezed into dime-store frames. What a dump.

"Would you wave a red flag before a bull?"

Woloski posed the question as he poured the guys tall glasses of

Crown Royal and Coke. He hadn't even asked them what they wanted to drink.

"My friends, one needn't flaunt one's wealth. It could . . . irritate our noble police officers."

Woloski smiled his black smile, set the bottle down and folded his thick, sausage-like fingers together on his lap. They were sitting around a chipped oak table in what was supposed to be the dining room.

When Woloski invited them for dinner, it must have been a figure of speech, because the only thing on offer was the rye. And now the man just sat and stared at them.

Fucking Yves, thought Kevin. Had to make that crack about the carpets when they came in. The wise-ass. Now Woloski was pissed at them. He gulped down his rye. He looked at his friends. They looked equally uncomfortable. Everyone but Marc had finished his drink. And no one was saying anything. Fuck.

Woloski finally broke the silence.

"I guess you're wondering why I asked you here."

The guys nodded.

"I know your work in the drug stores with the cigarettes. The word is that your work is clean, quick and professional. More important, you're still together. You obviously trust each other and can work together. I like that."

Woloski paused, then leaned forward to refill their glasses.

Marc couldn't contain himself.

"How the hell do you know our work? What the fuck is this?"

Woloski smiled again.

"Thank you, Marc. You've reminded me of something."

A black-haired teenager appeared at Woloski's side with a stack of files. Woloski opened the first one and began reading.

"Kevin Grandmaison, also known as Kevin Hart. Born on October 24, 1967. Mother, Marilyn Grandmaison, deceased. Father, Rick Grandmaison, now living on Caldwell Avenue, several convictions for drinking and driving. Also has a stepfather, Ron Hart. Attended Sir Robert Borden High School, then Ottawa Technical High School where he received his diploma. Current address, 1425 Zephyr Avenue, an apartment he shares with long-time girlfriend, Sylvie Guttadauria."

Woloski stopped reading and slid the file over to Kevin. Inside were colour photographs of him and Sylvie, Sylvie's mom, and his step-dad. There was even the mug shot of his father when he'd been arrested for drinking and driving a couple of years back. There were also copies of his birth certificate and report cards and pages of other information.

Kevin's heart felt like it wasn't beating.

Woloski had already opened the second file and was reading.

"Yves Belanger. Born February 22, 1973.

School: Woodroffe High School. Never received his diploma. Current address: 1125 Pinecrest . . ."

Kevin looked over at Yves. He was pale.

Woloski finished reading out Yves's file and then started on Tyler. Marc was last. When it was over, no one spoke. Yves had regained some colour and reached for the Crown Royal. He poured himself a very tall glass and handed the bottle to Kevin.

Woloski leaned in and spoke in a low, steady voice. "I know your credentials. I am positive you know mine. Now, let's cut the crap and do some business."

Tyler was still scanning his file. He let out a low, long whistle. "Mo-th-er-fu-ck-er."

It took Woloski less than 15 minutes to lay out his proposal. He had a friend who'd left a high-ranking position within a major drug-store chain. The bottom line was that there was some serious money that was ripe for the picking inside drug stores. They were so concerned about addicts busting in to get the pharmaceuticals, they over-loaded the security on that end of the floor. The safe was usually neglected.

If a team could get inside and crack a safe, they could walk away with as much as $50,000 in cash along with another $50,000 in stamps and lottery tickets. Woloski wanted Kevin, Yves, Marc and Tyler for the jobs. He would set them up and co-ordinate them. He would also train the gang on the basics: safe-cracking, how to disable alarms, how to pick locks.

In return, for every job set up by Woloski, the guys would have to give him a 25 per cent cut of the score. More important, the stamps, traveller's cheques and lottery tickets would move through Woloski.

He would give them 50 per cent of face value. The stamps were most important. No one seemed to realize what an easy target they were. A book of 10 sold for $4.20 and was almost as thin as a bill. You could fit $5,000 worth of stamps in a shoe box, so they were easy to get in and out of stores. And there were more than enough store owners who were eager to buy discounted stamps.

The guys were allowed to do as many jobs as they liked on their own, but with one condition: no matter who organized the job, the stamps and lottery tickets always must be moved through Woloski. The guys could keep the entire score on their own jobs.

"Realistically, I think you four combined could bring home a tenth of a rock a month," concluded Woloski.

A tenth of a rock. For the second time in minutes, Kevin's heart felt like it had stopped. That was $100,000. That was $25,000 a month each. Holy shit.

It was silent again. Marc pounded back the last of his drink and began chewing the ice. Woloski let the silence hang for 30 seconds, letting what he'd said sink in.

"I don't want an answer tonight," finished Woloski. "I want one tomorrow by noon. Okay?"

The guys looked at each other. No one said a word. But each one nodded. As they got up to leave, Woloski reached into a cabinet and pulled out an unopened bottle of Crown Royal. He pressed it into Kevin's hands.

"Thank you for coming, gentlemen."

They shook hands and thanked him for his hospitality. Woloski closed the door.

Y Y Y

The music was pounding, but Yves was a heavy sleeper.

He was face down on the bar at Auzone, a puddle of drool collecting under his chin and a large army of empty shooter glasses standing guard.

Kevin shook him.

"Yves buddy, come on. Wake up. Yves, buddy."

No answer. The guy was gone. Yves would do this, just drink as much as he could, as fast as he could, like he was trying to kill himself every Friday and Saturday night.

Kevin reached into his pocket and pulled out his wallet. He gave the bartender $200.

"Take care of him."

The bartender nodded so fast he almost sprained his neck.

"Yes sir."

Kevin veered out onto the dance floor to see if he could find Marc. He stood up on his toes. Holy shit. The bastard was dancing with this blond model-type and he had his hand down her pants. Kevin could see a thin strip of pubic hair as Marc was groping further down. Unbelievable. The fucking guy.

Over on the other side of the dance floor were two of Yves's buddies, Eric and Tim. They were pounding back beers and checking out the women. Kevin caught Eric's eye and shouted over to him.

"Hey! Yves is passed out at the bar."

Eric started laughing. He had been hanging with Yves for years and knew the guy could get out of control. They had been down to Mexico a couple of months ago and Yves had been so drunk, he fell down a flight of 40 stairs and tumbled out onto the dance floor. Amazingly, he didn't even spill all of his drink, and he just got up, downed the rest of his rye and started dancing. Eric threw his hands in the air and shouted back to Kevin, "That's my boy!"

Kevin raised his glass to Eric and Tim, then turned back and headed for the booth where Tyler was sitting. He was sitting with two women, and you could barely see the table for the number of drinks on it. Whoa. Tyler had his hand on the brunette's leg and was leaning in to kiss the other woman, a black girl with short, cropped hair. Kevin stopped in his tracks. He didn't feel like intruding quite yet. Tyler was looking pretty happy.

Instead, Kevin spun around and headed for the bathroom at the back of the bar. It had been a crazy night so far.

They had been at Woloski's during the day, picking up some blueprints of drug stores and getting some tools. Yves and Tyler had left early, just after 3 p.m., but Kevin and Marc had stayed late to get another lesson on how to disarm and open safes.

They had gone through it twice more, with the guys learning what wires to clip and where the safe was weakest structurally.

Woloski was a good teacher. Better than any Kevin had in school.

In all they had spent two days with him, first at his house then at a garage downtown he used as a safe house. After Woloski had gone through a job step by step with them, the guys were actually amazed. The jobs were pretty simple. If you knew when the money was going to be there and how to disarm the safes, almost anyone could do them. Check that. Anyone who was young and strong. They were all roof-entry and required a lot of climbing and crawling. Woloski had been pleased that the guys were all working out regularly. You needed to be agile and strong to get the work done.

The first job was already planned for next week, a Pharma Plus on Iris Avenue in Ottawa. They had everything they needed and everyone agreed it should pose no problem. It had been an exciting week.

After leaving Woloski's house and the phantom dinner last week, they had talked over his offer for all of five minutes in the car. There was no question about what to do. They wanted in.

"That was like something out of a movie. This is fucking great," Yves had summed up in the car going home that night, after taking several swigs out of Woloski's complimentary bottle of rye.

They had called him back the next morning like he asked and set up an appointment for their briefing. Since then, the guys couldn't stop talking about how many scores they could pull. Kevin swung open the bathroom door and headed for the urinal.

Today was really the last time they would ever see Woloski. He would get word to them about upcoming jobs through an intermediary and they would leave his cut of the take along with the lottery tickets and stamps at one of his safe houses. It was one of the ways Woloski protected himself.

Before Kevin and Marc had left him this evening, Woloski had shaken their hands and left them with a simple message: be good to me and I'll be good to you.

He then pushed an envelope into Kevin's hands. Inside was $10,000 in cash. "Just for good feelings. Have fun tonight, on me."

And then they had. Judging by Yves, too much.

Kevin stepped away from the urinal and zipped up his pants. He turned to the mirror and checked out his hair and straightened his black Armani blazer. He had picked it up last week from Harry Rosen and it hung well on him. He smiled. At $1,200 it should.

They must have spent half of Woloski's money already. They had taken their girlfriends out to a big dinner at the Lone Star, celebrating a big win at the casino, or so they told them.

Afterwards, they had stuck the girls in a cab and headed for the bars to celebrate in earnest.

All of them could drink hard, but with a $10,000 gift they were pushing their own limits. And the limits of the dozen or so girls they were supplying with booze as well.

He left the bathroom and checked his pager for the basketball scores before picking up another drink from the bar. Yves was still comatose. But the bartender was hovering around him, making sure no one sat too close or bothered him. The beauty of money, thought Kevin.

Marc was nowhere to be seen. He had probably taken that blond out to his car or back to his apartment. Probably getting quite a ride right now.

He looked over to where Tyler was sitting. What the? He was alone now. And he was waving Kevin over.

"What happened to the babes?"

Tyler shrugged. "They're meeting me back at my house in an hour. They wanted me to pick up some special refreshments first, if you know what I mean."

Kevin nodded.

"Anyway, I wanted to talk to you first."

Kevin sat down and looked into Tyler's eyes. He looked worried. Worried in a drunken-stupor and kind-of-horny way, but worried nonetheless.

"What's up, Ty?"

Tyler looked down at the table and reached for a drink, but stopped. He looked up and put his hand on Kevin's arm.

"Do you think we're going too far?"

Kevin nodded slightly. He knew this was going to come up sooner or later.

Y Y Y

It was the end of March and still pretty damn cold, -15°F at least.

Kevin and Tyler were walking down Promenade du Portage, Hull's main strip. Over a six-block span, there were more than 50 clubs or restaurants that served alcohol, complemented by dozens of late-night sub and donair joints to feed the drunken masses.

Drunken masses were a huge industry for Hull, what with the later closing hours for bars and the thousands of hooligans from Ontario eager to drink the night away.

Kevin pulled his blazer tight around him to try and warm up. He was beginning to wish he hadn't pulled Tyler out of the bar, but if they were really going to talk they didn't need the music, women and booze to distract them. Kevin shivered. Besides, the cold air would help sober them up.

Tyler was worried about taking the next step. And Kevin couldn't blame him. They had done a lot of work together in the past three years, probably 200 cigarette jobs plus 100 other break-ins, smash-and-grabs or peekaboos. But despite the hundreds of thousands of dollars they netted, it still seemed pretty tame.

It *was* tame, Kevin thought. They never had to worry about heat. Their jobs were small time. The police didn't have the time or the money to worry about them.

They were just four friends, all young — hell, Yves and Marc had just turned 20 — doing some small-time shit. If they ever got caught doing a cigarette job, they would likely only get a slap on the wrist, certainly no jail time. They could explain it to their friends and parents as a dumb mistake, something stupid they tried once and been burnt. After all, hiding in a drug store, smashing the window of a ski store or squeezing through the cooler of a Mac's Milk — that didn't exactly put you in the same league as a serial killer.

But going through the roof of the store, disarming expensive alarm systems and cracking safes — that wasn't kid stuff. That was serious crime. It'd be hard to explain that to Mom or Dad as a youthful lark. And police wouldn't look as kindly on them if they were caught with burglar's tools, decked out in black clothes and digging through the roof of a store. Or driving away with $50,000 in their pockets. No slap on the wrist, just a kick in the ass straight to jail.

Then there was the idea of working with Woloski.

The guy was big time. If something went wrong, he didn't just laugh it off. He took action, drastic action. None of the guys wanted to find out if the rumours about Drew Edwards were true.

Tyler stopped and leaned against the wall. He didn't get into this to end up with his various body parts discovered in some Ottawa suburb, another unsolved homicide.

"I'm all for this, man," he said. "I want the money, for sure. I'm just thinking: Do we really want to get involved in this shit? I mean, look. If we start doing this . . ."

What was next?

Kevin had asked himself that question a thousand times. He wondered if he'd ever lead a normal life or get a normal job. He didn't want to do this his whole life. Fuck that. He kept telling himself he was going to set up a nest egg then get out, maybe open a restaurant or a bar. A restaurant or a bar with a really good safe.

The thing was, he figured he had earned more than $200,000 in the past three years and he didn't have a thing to show for it. A nice Mustang. Good memories. A couple of thousand in GICs. But no fucking chunk of money to start up a business. It was the gambling and the partying that ate it all away.

If he didn't start saving, it was hard to think about life ever going back to normal. After all this, he wasn't going to get out of the business without something hard to show for his time.

Kevin sighed and looked up at the sky. Clouds were just parting and the moon was beginning to shine clear.

Really, their lives hadn't been normal since they started the cigarette jobs. Kevin hadn't had any kind of real job since he graduated from Ottawa Technical High School in 1987. With the cigarette money, all he did pretty much was do the scores, work out at the gym and hang out with the guys or Sylvie. Lots of trips to do cigarette jobs out of town or down to Windsor to blow a bundle at the casino. A couple of trips to Mexico. But no real work or school since he left Ottawa Tech. Nothing normal.

The same with Tyler. He finished up at Woodroffe in 1991 and had started at Carleton University the next year. He got a couple of credits but never returned. It was pretty hard to concentrate on the books when you had the kind of juice going that they did. Tyler was making more than most of the professors anyway.

The last real job Tyler had held was at that shitty gas station.

They at least had finished their high school. Marc and Yves were only 17 when the big cigarette money started to come in. They didn't really see much point in going to school. Marc left Woodroffe after Grade 11 while Yves was forced out a bit earlier. Yves had a disagreement with a math teacher that ended up with the teacher on the floor with a bloody face. Yves got suspended and didn't return.

Marc, he'd never held a real job. Sure, he waited tables or tended bars once in a while to help out friends. He was tight with almost every bar owner in the Market. But hell, how could someone work for a lousy hundred dollars a day when it was so easy to steal it?

Yves was 15 when he last worked, as a busboy at Peter's Pantry, a restaurant in west-end Ottawa. He lasted two months and never went back. Well, that wasn't quite right. Peter's Pantry had an off-track betting service, so guys would come down and bet on the horses from races in Miami, New York and Toronto. Sometimes the restaurant had as much as $10,000 in cash in its back room. One night last fall, Yves and Marc had done a little job on the place. They walked with $2,500 each.

"That's for paying me $5.25 an hour, motherfuckers," Yves laughed.

As they joked about the old days, Kevin and Tyler ducked into an alley so Tyler could piss. It was better in there, the wind didn't cut through them, thought Kevin.

The next step was really going to be the big time. If Woloski was right in his estimate, they would have five times as much money every month. It was a crazy concept.

As it was now, one of the hardest things was explaining the money the guys were constantly spending. Kevin's mom was dead, he had been on his own since he was 17. He wasn't that close to either his father or his stepfather, so they didn't ask questions. The only one he was accountable to was Sylvie, and he hid most of it from her. She never saw the money he spent drinking or gambling. When she asked where the rent and grocery money came from he made up excuses or said he'd won big at the casino. She was suspicious, but still wasn't saying anything.

Tyler and Marc lived together and just told their parents they had part-time jobs working as waiters. That explained the loads of cash and late nights when phone calls weren't answered. Marc told his girlfriend, Terri Anne, that he had won a big score —$60,000 — gambling and they were living off that. She was completely in the dark. Tyler's girlfriend, Kerri, seemed to know a little bit more, but she never asked questions. That was important. When the girls were getting expensive jewellery and a couple of trips a year to Jamaica or Mexico, they didn't ask any really tough questions.

Yves, he kept it pretty quiet. Most of his money went to gambling or partying, so it wasn't like he was bringing home a new big screen TV every night. His mom and girlfriend didn't really suspect much.

Tyler finished peeing and then looked up. His face looked sullen. It seemed he had aged 10 years in the last couple days.

"Am I being crazy to worry?"

"No man. You're right. If we go too far into this, we could be fucked. But what else are we going to do? Are you going to move back home with your mom and go back to university? What about me? Become a cook for a lousy $300 a week? What choice do we have?"

Kevin put his hand on Tyler's shoulder.

"Look, you can back out anytime you want. But give it a try. We just have to be smart enough to know when to stop. We'll get some money in the bank, then call it off. So long as we don't get greedy, we'll be fine. It's all about knowing when to stop."

They laughed.

"Tyler, think. Two years at this. A couple jobs a month. Just as long as we play it safe, just like Woloski's laid it out for us, we'll be fine. Then, two years from now, we'll be able to retire. Freedom 25. This is a once-in-a-lifetime gig," Kevin finished. He stared at Tyler in the crisp winter night, Tyler's face lit by the surreal glow of nearby orange street lights, Kevin's eyes full of sincerity.

"Now, how about inviting me back to your place with those lovely women?"

Tyler rolled his eyes. "Can you spell 'Fuck you?'"

"All right, all right."

Tyler hailed a cab while Kevin headed back to Auzone.

Y Y Y

Marc and Yves just sat and stared at the pile of money on the table. Even though they had been working for years, they had never seen such a stack. Usually they stole merchandise or cigarettes and then fenced it, getting their money in small chunks. If they took cash, it would just be whatever was in the till, maybe $4,000 or $5,000. Now, sitting on the table in Yves's apartment was $31,000, mostly in $20 bills.

"This is good."

Marc was straightening the piles on the table, rearranging them, like Lego bricks, with an unlit cigarette clenched between his lips.

The job had been easy. Too easy, almost. Everything had been where Woloski said it would be. They had arrived at the Pharma Plus at midnight and had been out at 2:30 a.m.

Yves and Marc almost couldn't understand it. Why weren't more people doing it? Why were drug stores so fucking stupid to leave their safes so vulnerable? How had they been so lucky to stumble into this kind of work?

Yves picked up a bundle of $20 bills and stuck his nose deep inside. It smelled so good.

"Yee-fucking-haaaaa!"

Yves was screaming. Fuck his neighbours. This was the greatest night of his life. Check that — greatest night of his life so far. The grin on his face was so big, and so happy, it seemed like Yves would never stop smiling. They'd just discovered the secret of life and they felt like they could ride it forever.

It was now just after 3:30 a.m and their work was done. Kevin and Tyler had left to make the drop — $10,000 in stamps —at Woloski's safe house. He had told them they could wait until morning, but they didn't want to make him worry. The four could split what was left on the table and Yves and Marc were dividing it into four piles.

Yves had already earmarked some of his score. Ten minutes after getting back from the job, he had called his bookie. It was the NCAA Final Four and on Monday night the University of Arkansas Razorbacks were going up against the Duke University Blue Devils in the finals of the college basketball championship. Yves had put $5,000 on Duke to win.

"Money in my pocket," Yves had boasted after Marc looked at him skeptically. "Trust me."

They had a police scanner going on the table and there hadn't even been a report of an alarm at the Pharma Plus. The cops wouldn't even know about the job until the employees arrived in the morning to find a hole in the roof and the safe jimmied. They had another job scheduled for next week and a couple of dozen more in the works for the summer. Hell, they could think of a hundred places in Ottawa alone they could hit. This was the shit.

Yves went to the fridge, picked out a two-litre bottle of Coke and took a 26er of Canadian Club from the cupboard. He poured two drinks and passed one to Marc.

"Not too fucking shabby, eh?"

They clinked glasses and downed their drinks.

Life was starting to look pretty good.

Chapter FOUR

December 1994
Ottawa, Ontario

With a peek over his left shoulder to make sure Sylvie wasn't coming, Kevin reached up onto the top shelf of his closet and brought down a crumpled Loblaws brown paper bag from his hiding spot.

It was still three days until Christmas 1994, but Kevin wanted to give Sylvie a little something now. He was heading out with the guys again, this time for the whole night, and Sylvie was getting depressed. She needed something to perk her up. Besides, thought Kevin, the gang had been working the new drug store jobs for more than eight months and the money was coming in like never before. He could afford it.

He reached into the bag and pulled out a stack of $50 and $100 bills. He quickly counted out $5,000 and set it aside on the bed. Kevin took another look inside the bag — there was lots left — and pushed it back up into his hiding spot.

"Sylvie, come here."

She popped her head around the corner and Kevin smiled. They had been dating for almost 10 years, ever since he was 17 and she was 15. She was a sweet one and a looker too, with long auburn hair and bright eyes. And the poor girl, she still had no idea how he earned his money or what he did when he was on the road.

Kevin loved her for it.

"Hon, it's almost noon, so I have to go meet the guys. We're just going to go shoot some pool and watch some hockey . . ."

Sylvie looked down at her feet.

". . . but I wanted to give you something first." Kevin handed her the money.

"Holy shit, Kevin! What is this?" Her eyes were nearly out of her head.

"It's for you. Go out shopping or for lunch or whatever. Go have some fun. I've been doing really good at the casino lately. I've won some major bets and I wanted you to have something nice." He leaned in and kissed her on the forehead. "Okay. Now smile." He held her by the shoulders and looked into her eyes. She smiled.

Kevin checked his watch. "Okay, I've got to jet. I might be out late, but don't worry. I love you."

Kevin grabbed his leather jacket and picked up the keys to his Mustang off the dresser. This is perfect, he thought to himself. That should keep her happy for a while. Kevin didn't want any worries on the home front. Especially not this week. He and the guys were getting ready to do the biggest job of their lives.

Y Y Y

For the past eight months, they had done two dozen jobs set up by Woloski, mostly drug stores and mostly taking in about $30,000 for their share of the score. They had done jobs all over Ontario and Quebec, hitting drug stores that were within a four- or five-hour drive. Now the guys had the system down pat and were working well together. They were ready to go out on their own. They had some drug stores lined up, and they were going to try a new angle too. A grocery store. Their first solo job would be on New Year's Eve.

Kevin wheeled the Mustang out of the apartment complex's parking lot and headed to pick up Yves. The two would be going to Kingston for the afternoon to check out the Loeb store on Princess Street. They figured they could make even a bigger score at a grocery store this time of year. During the holiday season everyone and their mother was stocking up on Christmas treats and then preparing for New Year's Day. If everything checked out okay today, the guys would return to Kingston on New Year's Eve to do the job.

Yves was waiting out front of his apartment building on Pinecrest Road. He was wearing a light jacket, no gloves and no hat.

"What are you, fucking stupid?" Kevin asked as he opened the car door. "You're going to freeze."

"Yeah, yeah. Shut up."

The two spent most of the ninety-minute drive from Ottawa to Kingston talking sports. The NFL playoffs had just started and the hockey and basketball seasons were going full-tilt. For Kevin and Yves, who both liked to lay the bets, it was paradise. They probably spent $2,000 a week playing Pro-Select, the government's sports lottery, and another $2,000 or $3,000 playing with local bookies.

The big question right now was whether they'd still be able to legally bet basketball. Toronto was supposed to get an NBA team in the fall of 1995 and the league was asking the Ontario government to knock the games off the ticket so the NBA wouldn't be associated with gambling.

"Fucking goofs," concluded Yves as Kevin pulled off the 401 at the Kingston exit. "They should realize that if it wasn't for the money riding on the games, no one would even give a shit about them."

The two had been in Kingston together dozens of times, including just four days ago. On December 18, the gang had hit the Shoppers Drug Mart on Bath Road and gone home with $40,000 in their pockets. Kevin found a spot in the Loeb's parking lot and the two walked towards the store. They were both dressed casually, in khakis and button-down shirts, that was the name of the game. They didn't want to draw attention to themselves by dressing too well or too poorly.

Yves grabbed a cart and the two slowly wheeled it up and down each of the aisles, occasionally throwing in some crackers or a box of Raisin Bran to keep up appearances. The goal was to get a mental image of the layout and come up with a game plan for the job. They located any cameras or motion detectors, and made sure to stop by the doors and examine what kind of alarms were hooked up. They spent almost an hour in the store, paid $45 for the random groceries that were in their cart and returned to the Mustang.

It looked like it was going to be a straightforward job. The doors were alarmed but there weren't any motion detectors on the store floor. The safe was right at the front of the store, a huge eight-foot-high chunk of steel. There were magnet-based alarms on the door of the safe but Kevin was pretty certain he could deactivate those. It was a high ceiling — more than 20 feet —but in the front right corner there was the manager's office, raised off the floor, that could only be reached by a flight of steel stairs. If the guys came through the roof right on top of the manager's office, they could just walk down the stairs and wouldn't have to risk hurting themselves when they dropped to the floor.

It was looking good.

Kevin pulled the Mustang out of the lot and across the street so they could watch the store close. It was just after 4 p.m. so they had to wait more than two hours, sitting and shooting the shit in Kevin's car. When the last of the customers left, Kevin and Yves took careful note of what the employees did inside. They all left by the front door, which was good. Some food stores paid stock clerks to stay late and fill the shelves. That could be an annoyance.

When Yves and Kevin were satisfied with what they had seen, they headed to a bar for a drink. It had taken more than three hours but they were confident that when they came back to the Loeb late at night next week, it would be theirs. Theirs for the taking.

Y Y Y

"Look at these sales," cackled Marc as he wandered through the aisles of the Canadian Tire. It was December 27 and Marc and Tyler were shopping for supplies amidst the madness of a day-after Boxing Day sale.

The gang had agreed that December 31 would be the best night for the Kingston Loeb job. The store would be closed January 1, what with it being New Year's Day and all. That would mean no employees coming in early and as much time as the gang needed inside the store. Even better, the Kingston police would be so busy with stop checks for drinking and driving and controlling rowdy midnight revelers, there would no time for a suspicious cop to do a drive-by of the Princess Street Loeb. It was perfect. The take would be huge, the gang could count on that. People would be spending every cent they had on food for parties and mix for drinks. The safe was going to be loaded.

Marc stopped the cart in the tools aisle and he and Tyler picked up the standard equipment: One pickaxe, three crowbars, some flat-head screwdrivers and tin snips. Tyler then went to grab some flashlights and duct tape while Marc went to get the dishwashing gloves.

Sometimes, when they wanted a thrill, the guys would try and shoplift the tools. These days, with a wad of hundreds in their pockets, it didn't make much sense. It did get expensive though. As a rule, the gang always ditched their tools after a job. That meant three or four times a month they had to pony up $150 at the Canadian Tire for a quality set of tools.

Marc picked up an economy-sized pack of yellow dishwashing gloves. When the gang first started out, they tried all different types of gloves, everything from the thin-plastic surgeon's gloves to baseball batting gloves to the expensive leather driving gloves. In the end, they settled on simple dish gloves. They were cheap, they were thick and they had a great grip on them. Even better, they clung to their hands so they could still work their tools with precision.

Of course, it made them look downright goofy, what with their dark clothes and neon-yellow dish gloves, but fuck, figured Marc, this was work, not a fashion show. Tyler was at his side now with the tape and flashlights.

"Ready to go home?" asked Tyler.

The two were still sharing a penthouse apartment in the west end and ended up doing most things together.

"Let's go by Rick's first."

Rick was always connected and the two could pick up a chunk of hash for the afternoon. Tyler gave the thumbs up.

They headed for the front of the store, choosing the cash with cutest girl at it, even though it had the longest line. Marc patted his hair into place and paid for the tools. The cashier, a beautiful girl with long black hair that smelled like kiwis, was named Francine. Marc chatted her up even though there was a long line of customers behind him shooting dirty looks. She had great eyes, maybe a touch of Asian in her face. Tyler finally tugged Marc from the line, but not before he had made his play. Francine had a boyfriend. But she still gave Marc her number.

Y Y Y

Kevin pulled out $500 cash and gave it to the clerk at the Tilden Rent-A-Car. He never used a credit card.

"That covers the deposit, doesn't it?"

"Yes, Mr. Blonde."

It was Dec. 30 and they were renting a Nissan Altima for the job in Kingston the next night. As always, they used a false name, just in case they had to ditch the car while under heat.

They each had an elaborate set of ID, purchased for the low, low, price of $250. Kevin had a whole new set made up in the fall after he had seen the movie *Reservoir Dogs*, about a gang of supercool hoods who robbed banks. Each of the hoods was given a working name after a colour. There was Mr. White, Mr. Brown, Mr. Pink. The hard-case in the movie was named Mr. Blonde, so Kevin had a driver's license, a birth certificate and a health card made up under the name Greg Blonde. It was hot shit.

Since they had been taking the road trips to do the drug-store jobs, the gang had been racking up huge rental car bills. They would take a car for a 10-day drug-store spree in Quebec, bring it back and be faced with more than $1,000 in late charges. Kevin would always smile, throw down some cash and shrug.

"Business. What can you do?"

Kevin grabbed the keys from the clerk and walked out to the lot to pick up the car. It was a mild day for December with a fresh thin layer of white snow covering the cars in the lot. He walked over to Marc, who was going to drive Kevin's Mustang back home for him.

"All set, Mr. Blonde?"

Kevin smiled.

Y Y Y

Kevin woke up late on the 31st. The boys had been out at Auzone again last night and dropped a load. But it was a sweet night. So many beautiful women. It had been great. They all hooked up.

Kevin rubbed his head. Ouch. The price he paid for all the rye. He looked at the clock. Just after 3 p.m., still lots of time. He lay back in bed and thought of the girl who had taken him home. She was short and blond with a super-toned body. She worked out, you could tell. She had such tight little breasts, her nipples seemed to explode off of her chest. Tiffany. Wow.

Kevin wouldn't mind seeing her again. He wondered if he had remembered to write down her phone number. He had been so drunk, he couldn't remember much.

Whoa.

Kevin reached down between his legs and passed his fingers over his penis. He brought them to his nose.

Shit.

It was the oh-so-sweet smell of sex. And it was strong.

Had Sylvie smelled that when he got into bed this morning? This could be trouble. Whenever his escapades took him somewhere he shouldn't have been, Kevin made a point of washing up to dampen any suspicion on Sylvie's part. He must have forgotten. More likely, been in a drunken stupor. This was bad.

He snuck out of bed and jumped into the shower for a quick scrub down. Then he went to find Sylvie.

"Baby?"

She was sitting on the sofa, scratching a pile of scratch-and-win tickets. On their last job, they had scooped up about 10 rolls of lottery tickets, 5,000 in all. Kevin had taken about 500 for a Christmas present for Sylvie. She was still working her way through the pile.

"Hmmmm?" Sylvie looked up.

No anger. No hurt. Only that excited look in her eyes when she was playing bingo or doing the scratch-and-wins.

He was safe. "Just wanted to remind you about tonight. I've got to help Yves's friend move to Kingston, but I should be back in time to party." That was a lie. He'd be out all night for sure. But it was an innocent one. He had to pay the rent didn't he?

"I know," said Sylvie absent-mindedly. She was concentrating on the scratch-and-wins. "Take care."

Kevin went back to his room and slipped on an oversized Boss sweatshirt and a pair of jeans. He grabbed his knapsack with his working clothes and headed for the door.

"I'm just going to the gym first, baby."

Sylvie smiled and waved.

Y Y Y

Kevin, Marc and Tyler were waiting in the white Altima. Where the hell was Yves?

After leaving his apartment, Kevin had headed over to Marc and Tyler's place. The three then went to the gym for a two-hour workout and an hour on the sun bed to keep their tans sharp.

They had called Yves before they had left for the gym and he had promised to be ready by 9:30 p.m. It was now 10 p.m. and they were stuck outside of his apartment, no sign of the guy.

"All right, 10 more minutes and we leave."

Kevin was sitting in the passenger seat and staring out the window. He wasn't going to put up with this shit.

There was a rap at the window of the car. Yves.

"Sorry guys, fuck I'm sorry. I promised Tania I'd have dinner at her parents' house tonight and I couldn't get away. They were just yappin' and yappin'."

"Get the fuck in."

Yves, dressed in the same dark clothes as the others, hopped in the back and Marc pulled the car out onto the street. They were all set to go, with the tools in the back seat, all wiped free of fingerprints. They had the police scanner going in the back seat as well, just to monitor the locations of speed traps and alcohol spot checks. They didn't want to be pulled over with the tools in the car. Later on, the scanner would tell them how close the heat was to them.

They took Woodroffe Avenue down to Highway 16 and then connected on to Highway 401. By 11:30 p.m., they were in Kingston.

Marc slowly drove down Princess Street, Kingston's main drag. As they passed the bar strip, a tinge of envy shot through the car. There were some very fine women waiting to get into those bars, all dressed to kill for the big night. Very fine indeed.

"I'd have them all, baby. Every one of them."

Yves was shouting and stuck his head out the car window.

"Hey baby," shouted Yves. "I know I'm not milk, but I'd do your body good."

"Relax," laughed Tyler. "Later."

The Loeb was on the more industrial part of Princess, several blocks down from the bar strip, so there was hardly any traffic at this time of night. There was the Bachelor Hotel right next door and that's where Marc parked the Altima. Yves turned up the volume on the hand-held police scanner and the gang listened for five minutes to make sure they were picking up all the Kingston frequencies. Everything seemed clear, the usual calls for public drunkenness and assault. Nothing on Princess Street. That was good. Yves clipped the scanner to the waistband of his pants and got out of the car.

The car was always "home base" for gang, so it was important to park it at least a block away from the store they were going to hit. It not only looked suspicious if there was a lone car parked at a store in the middle of the night, but if the heat came down and they had to run, they would meet back at the car and then make their get-away. If the car was too close to the store, the police would be able to stake it out and the guys would be screwed, so they preferred to park either a couple of blocks away or in a busy parking lot if there was one nearby. The Bachelor Hotel was perfect.

They walked across the hotel parking lot and headed for the Loeb. The streets were quiet.

Everything was set.

Y Y Y

The shadows of the building fell hard against the pavement as the four men snuck around back.

There was some snow on the ground but it was still mild enough that their breath didn't fog. Kingston was always several degrees warmer than Ottawa. From the looks of it, the side of the building was dry, no ice. That would make things easier.

All four pulled out their yellow dish gloves and slid them on. Tyler set down the satchel of tools he was carrying and took out the first crow bar and heaved it up onto the roof. The rest of the tools followed, except for the pickaxe. It was too heavy to risk throwing up onto the roof. If it missed, it would make a hell of a lot of noise as it fell back to the ground. Tyler handed it to Kevin, who slid it down the back of his shirt.

Kevin jumped up onto the loading dock. He couldn't believe the gang's luck. The building had a thin metal ladder going up the back, probably there so workers could inspect the roof. This was going to be easy.

Kevin climbed up first, followed by Marc, then Yves.

Because the Loeb had huge picture windows in front, it meant the guys inside could keep an eye on the street. Tyler had the keys to the rental car in his pocket and was going to stay outside, close to the Altima just in case the guys needed a quick getaway. From his position by the car he could watch the back of the building and keep watch up and down Princess Street. If something was up, he would call Kevin on his cell phone with the warning.

Up on the roof, Kevin headed straight for the front right corner, looking for the spot where the manager's office would be. He stopped ten feet from the front of the building. This looked good.

Yves and Marc had been collecting the tools and came up behind him. Kevin got down on his knees and pushed away the loose gravel, clearing a spot of about two feet by two feet where they would work.

He nodded and handed Yves the pickaxe. Yves brought it down hard, five or six times, gouging enormous holes into the tar of the roof. The tar was thick and soft enough to muffle the sound of the blows. It was no worse than a rubber mallet pounding a two-by-four.

Then all three used the crowbars to pry away the three inches of tar that sealed the roof, exposing a patch of dull-gray roofing tin. Yves picked up one of the crowbars and thrust the sharpened edge through the tin, opening up a thin hole. Marc reached for the tin snips and began cutting open a large sheaf of the roof.

Even with the cool winter weather, Marc's face quickly began to shine with sweat. Cutting through the tin was the most awkward part of the job and after five minutes of the work, Marc's forearms were burning. Marc cut along three sides of the square patch and then Yves and Kevin bent the tin back to open up a hole in the roof.

Below the tin there was a layer of insulation and the roof beams, spaced several feet apart, more than enough room for the guys to slip through. They pulled out the insulation and Kevin lowered himself down, bracing himself against two of the roof's beams.

Now all that was between him and the manager's office were the cheap panels of the white gyp board ceiling. Kevin leaned head first into the hole with Yves holding his legs so he wouldn't fall. He reached down and carefully picked up one of panels then passed it up

Yves. It was a delicate operation. If you knocked the panel the wrong way and it fell to the ground, it could set off a motion detector, if by chance there was one in the office.

They were in.

Y Y Y

A camera. There was a camera in the corner.

"Holy shit!"

Kevin spun around, making sure his face wasn't in view of the camera's eye. He was standing on a filing cabinet in the manager's office having just slipped through the roof. After taking out the panel, he had poked his head through and looked for any motion detectors. There were none, but he had somehow missed the camera. Kevin swore under his breath. He needed to do something fast.

There. On the table. A box of plastic grocery bags. Kevin stepped down off of the filing cabinet and walked backwards toward the table, making sure his face couldn't be seen.

He pulled out one of the bags and slipped it over his head.

"I must look like a fool," Kevin muttered as he pulled out two more bags and went back to the hole in the roof.

"Guys, there's a camera in the office. Put these over your heads before you come down."

No answer. Then Yves spoke.

"You're fucking joking right? You're pulling my leg."

"No, I'm serious, I swear. Put them on."

Yves and Marc were still sceptical. Kevin was always pulling little jokes. The worst was last July. They were on a job in Pickering and Kevin had gone in first. He was already on the store floor when the others had come down. He warned them that there were motions in the aisles, two feet off the floor. Marc and Yves were forced to belly-crawl down the aisle to where Kevin was sitting. The guys could feel the aisle was wet, but thought nothing of it.

At least until Kevin started laughing. There were no motions. And they had just belly-crawled through a puddle of Kevin's urine.

"You motherfucker, Kevin," whispered Marc. "If you're setting us up again, I'm going to stick this crowbar up your ass."

Kevin stuck his head up through the hole, complete with bag. "I'm serious. Let's go."

Marc and Yves looked at each other and nodded. They put on the bags and slipped down into the office.

Y Y Y

Kevin reached into the safe.

Nothing.

Some old receipts, a payroll book and some empty envelopes. But no money.

He shrugged. It would have been a bonus anyway.

They hadn't expected to find a safe in the manager's office. When Kevin and Yves had been up to scope out the store the week before, they figured the huge steel safe at the front of the store by the customer service desk was all the store had — or needed. But right by the door, underneath the camera, was a small, brown metal safe, maybe three feet high. It was cheap too. No alarm and all Kevin did was slide the wedge of his crowbar in between the door and the frame and pop it open. It took all of five seconds. Five seconds wasted.

"Nothing here guys, let's go downstairs."

The door to the manager's office wasn't alarmed so the guys clambered down the steel staircase to the floor of the Loeb. Kevin and Yves hadn't seen any motion detectors last week, but Marc did a quick walk around, looking for the tell-tale glowing red lights. No sign. On the way back to the front of the store, he stopped by the cooler and picked out some cans of Pepsi for the guys. When Marc got back, he tossed one of the cans to Kevin.

"Careful Marc. The shatter guard."

Marc scoffed. Almost every drug store had security system call a "shatter guard" near their front window. It was geared up to detect the sound of breaking glass, so if some dumb thief tried to break the front window or if a bunch of drunk hicks started taking shots at the window with a .22, an alarm would sound and alert police. When inside a store, the guys had to be careful not to knock anything glass if they were near a window, because it could trigger the alarm. But there was no glass around now and the Pepsi can was aluminum.

"It's a fucking can of pop. Take it easy."

Kevin ignored him, turning his attention to the safe. They had already put a table against the window so that if anyone drove by the parking lot, they could duck down and hide.

The safe was huge, eight feet high, and it looked liked it weighed 1,000 pounds. Kevin got to work on the alarm immediately. It was a standard, magnet-based alarm system, with the breakers actually on the outside of the safe. It was simply too easy.

There was one magnet on the top right-hand corner of the door, on the opposite side from the hinges. The sister magnet was just an inch away, on the frame of the safe. Both magnets were screwed onto the safe and were connected by wires to the alarm box on the wall.

It was a simple design. If the door of the safe was opened, it would break the magnetic plane and set off an alarm.

So all Kevin had to do was make sure the magnets were never separated and he was set.

He took out the roll of duct tape and stripped off several eight-inch-long strips. He carefully laid the tape across the magnets, making sure they were tightly bound together. He patted down the tape and jiggled it with his hand. It was solid.

Then he took the screwdriver and began to remove the magnets from the safe. First he took out the screws and then used the screwdriver so he could pry the magnets off and break the adhesive glue that also held them to the side. First came the one on the door of the safe, then the magnet mechanism on the frame. The whole time they remained taped tightly together. Once the magnets were off, Kevin followed the wires along the body of the safe, using the screwdriver to pop the wire out of its moorings.

When he was done, he was left holding the two magnets, taped together, with wires dangling from each one and connecting to the alarm box on the wall.

He stuck the wad of tape and the magnets against the wall.

"No one's going to steal that wall."

The job was done. The safe was clean.

They could take the pickaxe to the safe now and nobody would be the wiser.

Y Y Y

Yves was sitting against the front window. A fine sheen of sweat coated his forehead.

"Holy shit, that's one tough safe."

They had never broken into a safe that big before. First, they tipped the safe over onto its back and attacked it in the usual way. They each took their crow bars and slipped the wedge in between the door and the safe. And then they had pulled. And pulled. And nothing.

They had been at it for 30 minutes and the door hadn't even given any indication of coming loose. Yves had tried to peel back the outside metal and get at the casing, but it was impenetrable. They had tried to slip the lock mechanism out of its cylinder but that didn't work either.

"What are we going to do?"

Yves was talking to Marc. Kevin had disappeared into the back of the store, hoping to stumble on something that would help them.

Whenever a safe gave them problems in the past, the safes were usually small enough that the three of them could drag it out of the store and throw it into the car. Then they could take it back with them to Ottawa and work it over with a circular saw.

They couldn't move this one two feet.

Yves took a sip of his Pepsi and checked his watch. It was 2:30 a.m. They had been working for more than two hours. He looked up to see a block of wood sliding towards him. Then another. And another.

"What the . . . ?"

Marc and he stood and then they saw Kevin running towards them with a skid loader.

"All right, boys. I got us a plan!" roared Kevin.

He arranged the blocks of wood on the floor beside the safe.

"Okay, let's see if we can lift this thing up high enough to slip the wood under."

Yves and Marc looked at each other and shrugged. They all got on one side of the safe and got ready to lift. Kevin had a block of wood by his foot, ready to slide it under the safe if they got it up.

The guys were all built. They worked out at least four times a week and had muscles that would not have been out of place among a room of professional football players. But 1,000 pounds of safe was something else.

It wasn't even moving.

"I can't get a grip."

Marc was flexing his fingers inside the yellow dish gloves.

Kevin grabbed one of the crow bars and was able to just slide the flat tip under the safe. He pushed down. The edge of the safe came up a fraction of an inch.

"Yves buddy, can you guys get your fingers under there?"

Marc and Yves reached under the safe. Veins bulged out on their necks and forearms. The safe was up an inch. Now two. Kevin slid the blocks underneath.

"Okay drop it."

Marc and Yves stood back and admired their work while massaging their aching arm muscles. Kevin went and got the skid loader.

It fit snugly under the safe.

"All right boys, here we go. This is great."

Kevin pumped the handle a couple of dozen times and the safe was off the ground. They could roll it anywhere in the store.

"Yeah, great," said Yves. "But now what?"

Tyler's phone rang.

"What the fuck?"

He was leaning against the Altima with a map folded out across the roof, hoping to look inconspicuous. These were the guys' work phones and they were the only ones who had the numbers. It must be Kevin. There could be a problem.

"What?"

It was Kevin.

"A truck? How soon?"

Tyler hung up. Shit.

They needed a pickup truck, a half-ton if possible. And they needed it 10 minutes ago. Shit. What was going on in there? Why the hell a pickup? Tyler was worried. He checked his watch. It was 3 a.m.

Shit.

Where was he supposed to get a truck at this time of night?

He jumped up and down to try and get his blood moving. He had been waiting outside for two hours and he was damp and cold. Now he needed to work, fast.

Tyler leaned into the back seat of the Altima and dug under the seat. The guys always brought some extra tools just in case, and Tyler quickly found what he needed. A heavy flat-head screwdriver with a long handle. It wasn't the best thing for the job, but it would work. It would have to.

He scanned the parking lot to see what other cars were around. There was a red Jeep Cherokee but Kevin had insisted on a pickup truck with a big bed and no cap. The Jeep wouldn't do.

Tyler jogged out onto Princess Street and looked up and down the long street. There were cars parked along the road, but all sedans, Hondas and Toyotas, no trucks.

All the bars had let out so the parking lots downtown would be empty. He couldn't even call a cab, he'd look like a heatbag.

What would he tell the driver? I'm just looking for my friend's pickup? Besides, it was New Year's Eve. He would have better luck finding a truck dealership open than an empty taxi.

He checked his watch. Five minutes had passed. This was getting urgent.

He began to run down Princess, taking long, hard looks up each side street in search of the tell-tale shape of a pickup truck. For three blocks nothing.

"Fuck me."

Tyler was sweating. This was shit. He couldn't let the guys down.

Next block.

Nothing.

Next block.

There. Halfway up.

It was definitely a truck, looming in the driveway of a red-brick house. A white GMC Sierra.

Yes!

Tyler reached into his pocket and pulled out the screwdriver and walked up beside the truck. The door was unlocked. He eased inside, closing the door after him and leaning down on the bench seat so he couldn't be seen from the street. His heart was pounding, but he wasn't worried now. This would take about 30 seconds. When he and Marc were bored, they would steal cars together all the time and race them up and down the Queensway. It was a cheap high.

Tyler used the screwdriver to pop the casing off of the steering column. He leaned under and tugged the wires out so he could see their colours in the light of the moon. He yanked out the yellow and white wires, twisted them together and the ignition roared.

The sweet sound of the engine.

He peeked up above the dashboard. No lights had gone in the house. He checked his watch. Only nine minutes had passed. Tyler smiled. He was good. He pulled the truck gently out of the driveway and headed back to the Loeb.

Y Y Y

"Okay, Marc, when I say, all right. Ready?"

It was Kevin, from the other side of the huge sliding door.

Kevin and Yves were still inside the store with the safe on the skid loader. Tyler had the truck running and was backed up flush against the store's loading dock.

Marc stood outside the sliding door used to load shipments of groceries, getting ready to fling it open when Kevin gave the word. Marc had been able to disable the alarm on the small door, but the magnets for the huge sliding door were too high to reach. Marc had broken off the sliding door's lock with one of the crowbars and then come outside and got Tyler to pull the white GMC right up behind the loading dock. He had also taken the keys to the Altima from Tyler so he could run to the car as soon as the guys were ready to go.

The moment Marc lifted the door, an alarm would go off, so they wanted to time it perfectly, squeezing every second. Inside, Kevin and Yves pulled the skid loader about 20 feet away from the door so they could build some momentum as they pushed.

They took a deep breath and began to push it towards the door. It was building up speed.

"Now Mark, do it!"

Mark ripped open the door, sending it flying upwards. The alarm bells roared, piercing the quiet night.

Yves and Kevin had the skid going right for the back of the truck. Boom. The truck almost buckled under the sudden weight of both the safe and skid loader.

Kevin and Yves jumped off the loading dock, slammed the tailgate closed and hopped into the truck. Tyler peeled out of the lot, the safe along with the skid firmly in place, and Marc sprinted for the hotel parking lot and the safety of the Altima. The alarm bells were still screeching.

As the truck roared down Princess Street towards the 401, Yves pounded his fists against the dash board.

"Holy motherfucker!"

They were blocks away and they could still hear the bells going. Marc had agreed to take a different route to the 401 so the truck was the only vehicle on the road.

Tyler looked over at the other two.

"Good work. How close do you think the cops are?"

Kevin shook his head.

"No idea."

Ten minutes later they got their answer.

They were on the 401, heading back to Ottawa when the scanner crackled to life.

"There's been a report of a 10-34 at the Loeb grocery store on Princess Avenue. Could we get two units to report. I repeat, the alarm company has notified us of a 10-34 at the Loeb grocery store at 1225 Princess Street. Two units needed immediately."

Kevin and Tyler looked at each other and started laughing.

The 10-34 was the police code for a break-in. The cops had just got the call now. They hadn't even been to the store yet.

Kevin looked in the rear-view mirror. The road was empty and the lights of Kingston were just a faint glow in behind them.

Kevin laughed again.

"This is just too fucking easy."

Y Y Y

Forty minutes out of Kingston, the stolen Sierra was running near empty.

"Let's push it and try to make it back to Ottawa," Yves said.

"We're never going to make it, there's no *way* we're going to make it on what's in the tank," Tyler argued, glancing over his shoulder. "Especially with this load. There's no way."

Kevin, sitting between them, figured they had two options. Stop for gas with a thousand-pound safe which was far from inconspicuous in the back, or run out of gas on Highway 16 back to Ottawa, and freeze to death in the dark waiting for help with a thousand-pound safe in the back of the truck.

"Let's stop."

Tyler looked at Kevin. The quick getaway from the slow-footed Kingston cops seemed a lot less romantic right now. They'd have been to the store by now, and maybe got a report of a stolen truck.

He quietly pulled the Sierra into a gas station where the 401 and Highway 16 meet. Kevin stared straight at the attendant's booth. No other cars were at the station.

"Tyler you get out and pump the gas," Kevin ordered. "Yves, get inside and distract the guy. Don't let him look over here."

Tyler jumped out, and started with the gas. Yves went inside.

He went straight to the magazine rack on the far side of the small cramped store. He grabbed a Playboy, held it up, and asked, "How much?"

The attendant, who'd glanced at the truck when it pulled in, turned to Yves. "$5.95."

"And this one?"

"$3.50, sir."

Yves asked about two more, keeping the clerk's back to the truck. Tyler came in, paid for the gas, Yves bought a copy of *Sports Illustrated* and they left.

Pulling out, Kevin stared at the attendant, who stared right back. It was somewhere around 4 a.m., New Year's Day. Kevin smirked, winked, and the attendant turned away.

Y Y Y

It was starting to get light out when the guys finally got back to Ottawa. Marc had long since caught up with the truck, and the rented Altima was tight on their tail as Tyler negotiated the empty streets, heading for the autobody shop on Gladstone Avenue. It was one of the half-dozen safe houses Woloski kept in the area for his guys to use. Once they were inside, the guys would have as long as they wanted to pop open the safe.

Kevin hopped out of the car, punched the code into the electronic lock at the bay door and swung it open. The truck, the safe and Tyler disappeared inside.

Originally they had planned to leave the safe at the body shop, go home and catch a couple of hours of sleep before starting work on it. But there was still too much adrenaline flowing to sleep.

Kevin rummaged around the garage for the Quick-Cut saw and plugged it in.

"Let's do it boys."

They took turns cutting into the safe. Because there was a thick fire insulation in the walls of the safe, they had to leave the garage every half-hour to let the toxic fumes the saw spit up clear. After four hours of cutting, they were in.

Kevin pulled out six money bags and a dozen cashier's tills. They began to count.

Eighty thousand. And that was without counting the $1 coins or silver.

The guys had just made $20,000-plus each for a night's work. Marc ran his fingers through the piles of bills.

"Happy fucking New Year."

Kevin and Sylvie get married in Jamaica, 1993

Marc Flamini and Terri Anne, Jamaica, 1996

Mark Flamini, Cancun, 1995

Kevin and Sylvie at the Mirage Casino in Las Vegas, 1995

Yves Belanger with an unidentified girl in Cancun

Tyler Wilson, modelling shoot in Florida, 1996

Tyler Wilson in Florida

Kevin in early 1997

Chapter FIVE

January 23, 1995
London, Ontario

Kevin and Marc couldn't help themselves.

They had just hit three major jobs in three days — Belleville, Kitchener and, last night, London — and they couldn't resist. They dumped their bags of money on one of the hotel-room beds. It looked like a pile of leaves in fall.

Kevin went first. From the bathroom, he took a running start and launched himself onto the bed belly first. Bills flew everywhere.

Kevin was rolling around on the bed. They had counted it. Three times. They'd made $100,000 in three nights. This was just plain crazy. Yves and Tyler were already out at a bar. They were going to meet them there later. But first, business.

They piled it back up onto the bed and Marc took a run.

"Yes motherfucker!" he screamed as he soared onto the bed.

A knock on the door.

Kevin and Marc looked at each other. And smiled. Their party had arrived.

They quickly used the spare quilt to cover up the money, and Marc opened the door. There was a tall, red-haired woman in a tight, short black dress with tiny red-roses speckled on the fabric. It was low-necked, exposing a breath-taking amount of smooth cleavage.

"I'm Vanessa. I'm from Evening Fantasy Models. I'm here to meet two gentlemen. A Mr. Blonde and a Mr. White?"

Life was good.

CHAPTER FIVE

February 4, 1995
Acapulco, Mexico

Holymotherfuckerjesussonofabitchchrist.

Yves was in serious pain.

He had spent all day on the beach, working on his tan, but ended up burning the shit out of his chest and stomach. It was his first day in Mexico too, fuck. The four of them had come down as reward for their hard work. The other guys had stayed out just as long, but no one was as burned as bad as he was. And now he was paying the price for it.

He had picked up this wild chick from California at the News disco and now she was on top of him, riding him like a fucking cowboy. That was the good part. With each thrust of her pelvis, her enormous tanned breasts slapped hard against the sensitive skin of his chest. That was the bad part.

Yves tried to concentrate. Just block out the pain. He bit his lip.

Ouch.

It wasn't working.

He hadn't had enough to drink. The pain just wouldn't go away.

Fuck.

There was no way around it. Yves pushed the woman off him, dumping her on the bed, then gingerly pulled a T-shirt on.

"Sorry babe, this just isn't working."

He picked up her leather skirt, her black thong underwear and high-heeled pumps. He couldn't find her blouse or bra. He opened the hotel room door and threw her clothes into the hallway.

Her eyes were wide.

"You bastard."

She pulled herself up with as much dignity as possible and strutted out of the room. Yves just shrugged and started pulling on his pants. He would go back down to the bar, have another drink or six, enough to make him forget about his tender chest. Then he'd just pick up again. There were hundreds of hot women in the bar.

Yves grinned wide and headed for the elevator.

He loved Mexico.

February 12, 1995
Oshawa, Ontario

Marc looked over his shoulder to check on how Yves was doing at the safe.

Holy shit. Literally.

He had his pants around his ankles and his ass buried deep inside the safe. And it was starting to reek.

"You fucking pig!"

Yves grinned up at him.

"There was only $7,000 in here, the fucking pricks. It wasn't even worth our time. I'm just letting them know what I think." He reached into the money bag and picked out a fistful of $5 bills. He reached around to clean himself.

"Personal hygiene," Yves explained, grinning at Marc.

February 27, 1997
New York City, New York

The clerk sidled up beside Tyler.

"Beautiful, aren't they sir? Pure silk."

The clerk was right. He had never felt a tie like it.

"Only $350. It's an extraordinary buy. You'd spend twice as much for an inferior product at other stores."

Tyler laughed to himself. Only in Manhattan would a $350 tie be a bargain. There were eight or nine ties he loved. Shit, they'd be $2,700 altogether. And he already had dropped $1,000 on a pair of shoes and $5,000 at the Klein boutique.

Tyler gritted his teeth. He had to be more careful with his money. He would cut down.

He only picked up his six favourite ties.

"I'll take these. Cash."

March 11, 1995
Tweed, Ontario

They were cooked.

How the hell had they missed that motion detector? How long had the silent alarm been ringing?

Kevin and Marc were working on the safe when they got the call from Tyler. Six cop cars were coming into the lot. It was too late to get out. There was nowhere to run or hide. If they somehow got lucky, Tyler would have the rental car out at the gas station on Highway 7. He'd wait until dawn.

Kevin peeked around from the manager's office and looked out the front of the store. There were the cops. Fuck.

That bastard Yves. He picked a great time to take his girlfriend down to the Bahamas. He was going to come back and they'd all be nailed. He was going to laugh his ass off.

There was a crackle of a megaphone.

"We have the building surrounded. Come out with your hands up."

Fucking cops.

What to do.

Kevin peeked out a back window. There were maybe six cops out back and another 10 out front. And a small crowd was beginning to gather too. There were three bars on the block and maybe 20 or 30 drunken men had come out to watch the scene, attracted by the roar of the sirens and the brilliant flash of the police lights.

"Let's run for it."

Marc was wired, his eyes bulging as he shifted quickly from foot to foot.

"No way. We have to think."

Kevin had an idea.

"What if we can distract the cops?"

He had a plan. Kevin and Marc went to the back door. They could hear the barking dogs from the canine squad.

"We're going to count until 10 and then we're coming in."

The fucking megaphone again.

"Ten."

Marc and Kevin took a shopping car and loaded it with bottles of Scope mouthwash.

"Nine."

They went to the back door.

"Eight."

Kevin looked at Marc. Ready? he mouthed.

"Seven."

Marc nodded.

"Six."

Kevin rolled the shopping cart back from the door.

"Five."

He began pushing it. Hard.

"Four."

Marc kicked open the door as hard as he could. It smashed open and Kevin threw the cart out the back. It spun off the loading dock, sending bottles of mouthwash flying and spinning everywhere.

"They're coming out the back! They're coming out the back!" The cop was screaming into the megaphone.

Marc and Kevin ran to the front of the store. They could see through the window that the plan was working. All the cops from the front were running around back to help out.

Kevin picked up his crow bar and threw it into the front window, using every inch of his strength. It went scorching through, shattering the picture window and sending glass flying in all directions.

"They've got guns! They've got guns!"

Marc and Kevin were screaming it over and over at the top of their lungs as the jumped through the hole where the front window had been.

The crowd of onlookers freaked. Almost as one, they turned tail and ran out of the parking lot and up the street. Within seconds, Marc and Kevin had caught up to the crowd, a bunch of heavy-footed, drunken men. They slowed their pace so they'd stay in the group.

Kevin took a look over his shoulder. The cops were just coming to the front of the drug store now. They looked stunned.

Kevin and Marc took a quick left with five other men, then turned right up the next block. They stripped off their yellow gloves and dropped them as they ran. Next came their black shirts. Thankfully, they always wore a second, white shirt underneath. Just in case.

They ducked into a back yard and over a fence. Across another yard. There. An apartment building with dozens of cars in the parking lot. Marc slipped a screwdriver out of his pocket as they ran in. There. A Ford station wagon. Very inconspicuous. Mark had the lock popped and engine started in 15 seconds. He screeched out of the parking lot and headed out to Highway 7. He took a peek down the street. Cops with flashlights had stopped a group of men they had been running with.

They didn't speak until they were on the highway.

"That was too fucking close."

March 31, 1995
Cancun, Mexico

Tyler could not even see.

He groped his way along the bar and reached up for the clay bell. The bartender raised his eyebrows.

"You guys are fucking nuts man," he shouted with thick accent.

Tyler threw $1,000 U.S. down on the bar.

"I love you too," he slurred. He rang the bell.

The bartender shrugged his shoulders and reached for the microphone.

"The bell has been rung. Free drinks for everyone."

The bar was packed and everybody cheered.

Tyler fumbled his way back to the couches where the other guys were sitting. Trevor, Greg and Woody, three of the crew's friends, had also come down to Mexico for the trip, and they had been packing back the drinks too. Along with the men, there was a about a dozen very attractive young women, the types who become very interested when they saw what kind of money was being thrown around that night. It seemed every time one of the guys rang the bell, another girl or two would wander over to the table.

They had arrived at the bar just after 7 p.m. and it was now closing in on 3 a.m. By Tyler's best count, he had rung the bell six times. And the other guys were matching him ring for ring, 24 times in all.

They had just arrived in Mexico two days ago. After the scare in Tweed, everyone needed a holiday. Even Yves, who wasn't even there. The fucker.

It was hard convincing the girlfriends that the four had needed another guys-only holiday. But screw them. Two waitresses came by, their trays loaded with drinks for their table. The girls cooed with pleasure and Tyler checked the faces of the other guys. Nobody had passed out. Yet. But they were close.

He raised his drink. "Ready, boys?"

Yves looked up groggily and sneered at Tyler. "You bastard."

The four downed their drinks.

Tyler could barely feel his hands. He'd never been so drunk in his life. He closed his eyes. He was startled awake by the cheering of the crowd.

Kevin was at the bar, ringing the fucking bell again. Round 25.

The night was never going to end.

April 23, 1995
Chatham, Ontario

Marc cleared away the last of the insulation. They were through and it had taken less than 20 minutes. This was shaping up to be a good job.

It was another Shoppers Drug Mart and they expected no problems. The weather was mild this time of year in Chatham, and although there was lots of traffic on the streets below them, no one was coming into the parking lot or checking the roof.

Marc handed his crowbar to Kevin who was standing next to him. Yves was about 20 feet away, taking a piss against one of the duct vents protruding from the roof. Marc leaned down and with Kevin bracing his feet, hung so he could poke his head into the manager's office. No cameras. No motions. Marc shone the flashlight around the room. No nothing. As usual, the boneheads had the alarms outside the office.

Marc lowered himself down and began laughing.

"When are these guys going to learn? You have to put the alarm where the money is. It's so fucking simple. Alarm the money."

He dropped to the floor and went to the safe while Yves started to climb down with the bag of tools to break the safe.

"No way," Marc shouted. "You won't believe this."

Yves turned, his eyes wide with panic.

"What? What?"

Marc shone the flashlight on the safe's lock. Unbelievable.

"The key. The key is in the fucking lock." He bent down, turned the key and pressed down on the handle.

The door swung wide open.

Marc looked at Yves. Yves looked at Marc.

They started laughing. Yves buckled over. He could hardly breathe. This was the stupidest thing he'd ever seen. Marc emptied the safe, passed the bag up to Kevin. Marc quickly knocked twice on the wood desk, just for good luck and Kevin followed suit on the roof. Marc then kicked Yves, still laughing, "Come on let's go."

The take was huge — $45,000 in cash, another $15,000 in coins plus $20,000 worth of stamps, traveller's cheques and money orders.

Driving back to the hotel, Yves was still having problems understanding what had just happened. He ran his fingers through his hair, looking back down the street.

"That manager is going to get in *shit* tomorrow morning. What a fucking douchebag. Leaving the key in the lock."

May 11, 1995
Toronto, Ontario

Kevin didn't quite know how to handle the situation.

He had talked to some buddies and everyone said this dealership was totally down. Any car you want, no questions asked. Still, how exactly did one go about doing this?

He felt the bulge of money burning in his pocket. It was smart to buy it in Toronto in any case. Ottawa was too small, it would raise too much suspicion. According to his friends, there was so much loose money flying around Toronto, some businesses catered to it. This, apparently, was one.

Kevin braced himself and pushed open the glass door and walked in. Yves had been smart. He had bought a '94 Mustang Convertible last month, but had bought it used from a friend of Woloski's. Of course there were no questions asked when he paid in cash.

A preppy-looking salesman approached, wearing a sharp striped blazer and greasy smile.

"What can I do for you today sir?"

"I'm looking for a car. A Corvette."

The salesman nodded.

"Anything specific?"

Anything specific. Kevin almost laughed. Only the car that had been tattooed on his brain since he was old enough to dream.

"Midnight-blue convertible, fully loaded."

The salesman smiled and led him to the showroom. Kevin ran his hand along the smooth finish. It was the car he had always wanted. He had saved almost everything from the jobs during the past six weeks to get the $60,000 he needed to buy it.

"Beautiful isn't it?" The salesman gave Kevin a knowing smile. "If you want a test drive, we'd need a deposit. Store policy. You get a lot of dinks in here who couldn't afford a Hyundai and just want to get a cheap thrill with the test drive."

Kevin laughed. "Don't worry. I don't need a test drive."

He reached into his pocket and pulled out a brown manila envelope.

"Do you take cash?"

The salesman didn't miss a beat. His nose was twitching at the sudden scent of a huge commission.

Kevin stuttered a bit and started into his story . . .

"I won at the Super Bingo and . . ."

The salesman raised his hand.

"You don't have to explain sir. Let us just run the money over to the bank and we can have the car ready for you in an hour. Would you like something to eat or drink while you wait?"

Kevin couldn't believe it. The guys were right. This place was very good.

June 2, 1995
Ottawa, Ontario

Tyler passed the spliff to Marc and he took a huge, long drag. They were baked. Slumping into the couch, staring at the TV.

It was after 6 p.m. and they were unwinding at their apartment after a job had gone sour the night before. They had set off the alarms at the drug store in Gatineau even before they got through the roof and the four of them had had to bail quick. Their nerves were shot.

Kevin was back at his place with Sylvie. Some sort of penance for all the nights away, the nights without phone calls, the trips. All of it.

Marc stubbed out the joint and Tyler leaned forward to roll another one. On TV, the local news was going full tilt. They waited for the sports highlights to see who had won the afternoon baseball games. They had some serious money down.

Yves stumbled out of the kitchen, holding a bag of Doritos and some pancake mix. He wandered to the coffee table and set it down.

"Food."

Yves could barely speak and he was peering around the room with heavy-lidded eyes.

Marc began giggling. The idea of Yves making pancakes just seemed to be the funniest thing he'd ever heard.

"Blueberries," Marc said. "Yves!" He snapped his fingers, "I'd like blueberries with my pancakes!"

Marc got up out of his chair and started for the kitchen. He was hungry but he wasn't going to eat that shit. He could cook and was overcome by the urge for some penne pasta in a nice basil-tomato sauce with some fresh bread.

Tyler was packing the filter into another joint when he looked up at the TV. It was Crime Stoppers.

Holy shit.

"Marc get back in here. Look at that."

Even Yves turned around to watch the TV.

Crime Stoppers was re-enacting a break-in at the Shoppers Drug Mart on Merivale Road from a couple of months back. The thieves had gone through the roof. They even showed some fuzzy videotape from the security camera. If you looked hard enough, you could almost tell it was Kevin's ass in the lower left-hand frame.

"We're TV stars."

Tyler sparked the joint.

"Cool."

June 30, 1995
Montreal, Quebec

Kevin, Yves and Tyler snuck into the bathroom and gently closed the door.

Marc had just brought home a sweet one, maybe 19 and blond.

"I have the whole suite to myself, trust me," oozed Marc as he led the woman to the bedroom, massaging her shoulder and running his hand down along her waist. Soon they were on the bed, her dress unzipped, his hands all over her breasts and thighs. He slipped the dress over her shoulder and eased her underwear off her hips and down her smooth legs. He ran his lips along her nipples and eased her over onto her back. Yes.

The bathroom door opened. Marc saw it out of the corner of his eye. The girl was oblivious.

Yves crawled up beside the bed.

Marc could barely stop from laughing.

Yves ran his fingers along the girls back and thighs, then gently inserted his middle finger into the girl's rear. The girl gasped. Marc bit his lip.

Yves crawled back to where Tyler and Kevin were breaking up. He stuck his finger under Kevin's nose.

Tyler started howling.

He couldn't stop himself.

July 11, 1995
Gatineau, Quebec

Kevin bent down low against the plastic grass and tried to line up the shot. He would need to bank it off the wall to get around the plastic statue of Snoopy, making sure he hit the ball hard enough to carry over the three bumps that stood between him and the hole. Damn. It was going to be a tough shot.

"Just take the fucking shot. What are you? Arnold Palmer?"

Yves was standing beside the Snoopy statue with Woody, or Jeff as his parents named him. Woody was tight with all the guys in the gang and loved to place the bets as much as Yves and Kevin. He was the only one who would regularly join them on their trips to the Maxi Putt miniature golf course in Gatineau. It was a simple game. The three of them put in $1,000 each for the first nine holes and another $1,000 each for the back nine. Whoever completed the first nine holes with the lowest score got the $3,000, with the same going for the back nine.

Fucking Woody had won the first nine, finishing them up in 19 shots, and pocketed the three dimes. Kevin had done the course in 21 shots while Yves had totally screwed up on the windmill hole, taking six shots to get it down, and finished with a 25.

Now they were on the Snoopy hole, a par three. With only one hole remaining, Woody and Yves were tied with 17 and Kevin had 18. Woody and Yves had each shot a three on the Snoopy hole, and Kevin was about to take his second stroke. If he could make this shot now, he could pull into a three-way tie for the lead.

"C'mon, Kev. Take the shot. You know I'm going to take more of your money, so just hit the damn ball."

He was leaning on his putter and checking out some girls who were trying to manoeuvre the waterfall on the 15th hole. Woody was a good guy, he liked to party as much as the crew and even though he knew the gang was up to something illegal he never asked questions. Kevin liked him. But damn if he was going to let that fucker take his money again.

He stood up and got behind the ball. Crack. The ball veered off Snoopy's tail and bounced off the course onto the paved pathway. That was a two-stroke penalty.

"Fuck."

Kevin began to pound the Snoopy statue in the head with his putter. Flakes of white and black paint began to fly and the girls at the waterfall hole were staring at them.

Woody and Yves were still laughing as the manager escorted them from the premises.

July 23, 1995
Peterborough, Ontario

The fucking cop had his gun drawn. Now he was pointing it right at Kevin.

"You on the roof. Get down. Get the fuck down."

Kevin backed away from the edge.

Some dickwater cops had been driving by the drug store and saw their car behind back. Tyler had been smart and pulled away but the fucking cops had stuck around to check things out. Everything would have been fine, but Kevin made a dumb mistake. When he heard the noise, he snuck up close to the edge, to try and get an idea of where the cops were. They were right below him. And then one looked up.

Fuck.

Kevin could hear the cop calling for back-up.

"I repeat, you on the roof, get out where we can see you."

Holy fuck, holy fuck, holy fuck.

He crept slowly back to where Yves and Marc were standing. They had just started digging through the roof. Hell, they had been at it for maybe five minutes when the fucking cops showed. He should have waited before trying to check them out. He could hear sirens getting closer. Kevin's heart felt like it was about to vault out of his chest.

"Guys, they don't know you're here. Just lie down and I'll try to, uh . . ."

Kevin stopped. He didn't have a clue what he'd do.

"Just stay fucking quiet."

Three more police cruisers pulled into parking lot.

They had the megaphone out now.

"You on the roof. This is your last warning. Get out where we can see you."

Kevin walked closer to the edge again. Ohmygod. The cops were swarming.

He spun around. He wasn't going down in Peterborough-fucking-Ontario. Yves and Marc, lying beside the half-finished hole in the roof, were staring at him. Marc was pointing to Kevin's left.

Around the back there was an eight-foot fence separating the loading area from a farmer's field. It was only about 15 feet away from the roof.

Kevin closed his eyes, then moved towards the edge of the roof.

"Don't shoot," he said, peering over the edge. "I'm coming down the back. I surrender."

The cops still had three guns on him.

He circled to the back side. Halfway there, he started sprinting, kicking up the little pebbles that covered the roof. He was hurtling forward. His foot caught the top of the fence and he was spinning out of control. He landed hard in the field, right on his arm. It cracked with a sick sound and shivers of pain shot up his left arm.

"Motherfucker." He couldn't see straight.

The cops were shouting and pointing to him. Some were trying to climb the fence, others were running for their cars.

Kevin picked himself up and began to run, faster than he ever had before. He held his damaged arm to his chest, tears starting to trickle down his cheek. He headed for the road, then across to the highway and into a subdivision of suburban homes.

Six cops were in pursuit. Kevin never ran so fast in his life.

Back up on the roof, Marc smiled at Yves.

Every single cop had left to chase Kevin. They strolled to the edge of the roof and slid down the pipes. Then they walked out to the street, hotwired a car and drove home. Kevin's pain was their gain.

Twenty minutes of chase, followed by a clever duck-and-hide, left Kevin alone. He spent the night huddled in the garbage shed of a Home Hardware store. Shivering with pain, fear and cold, he passed out sometime around 4 a.m.

When he woke, light was breaking through the crack between His watch read 6:36 a.m. It sounded like everything was quiet. He peeked outside. Nothing. Kevin groaned as he pushed open the shed door, his arm swollen and throbbing. Beside the Home Hardware, an old Chevy Cavalier was parked. Kevin took off his shirt to muffle the sound of the car window smashing, and painfully slid into the car. Using a hammer he found in the shed, Kevin smashed open the steering column and quickly got the engine started.

His arm was in agony. He spent the drive back to Ottawa chewing Tylenols he picked up at a gas station and peering into the rear-view mirror to see if the police were on his ass. He needed to find a safer line of work.

August 3, 1995
Ottawa, Ontario

Marc and Yves were playing video games when there was the knock on the door. Marc flipped the pause button on NHL '95 and looked at Yves.

"That must be him."

The man at the door was thin and frail-looking, already going bald even though he couldn't have been older than 30. He looked nervous as Yves ushered him into his apartment. "You want a drink?"

He nodded his head vigorously. "Vodka, please."

Yves went to get the drink while the man set up his suitcase beside the video game on the table. It was Nathan, the brother of one of Yves's old high school buddies. He had been working with an alarm company for the past two years, doing installations and maintenance. According to Yves's friend, he was good at what he did. And, according to Yves's friend, he had suddenly become real hungry for money. A penchant for cocaine, apparently.

This kind of information would be helpful. They already practiced every second weekend, buying alarms from Canadian Tire for $200 or $300, then setting them up in the basement. The goal was to find different techniques to disarm them. And usually, the same principle worked on the small alarms as it did on the big ones. But this guy would know for sure.

"Look," the man said, having downed a triple-shot of Smirnoff in a single gulp. "I'm real nervous about this. This could mean my job, man."

Yves pulled out an envelope and passed it to him. The man thumbed through it, making sure all $2,000 was there. He calmed down considerably.

For the next hour he demonstrated his company's entire product line, pointing out each alarm's strengths and flaws. Most of it Marc and Yves already knew. One thing troubled them.

The man had described their new product that would be on the market in a couple of years. In response to so many magnet-based alarms so easily being disarmed by taping them together and removing them from the door or safe — Yves nudged Marc — they had improved its design. In the future, there would be mercury inside each magnet. That would mean the alarm would sound if the plane was broken, as usual, but also if the alarm was tilted or shifted in any way. It would be impossible to take them down. The alarm specialist gave a queasy smile. Then he packed up his bags and left.

After Marc had closed the door behind him. He turned to Yves.

"Nothing like new challenges." He flipped on the hockey game before Yves was ready and potted a quick goal.

August 23, 1995
Las Vegas, Nevada

Yves poked Kevin in the ribs. A gorgeous, blond woman had just passed Kevin a set of gold keys with dice on the key chain.

"The suite? They're giving you the suite? For free?"

Kevin smiled. "I told you buddy, I've been here before. Did you think I was lying?"

Indeed, Kevin had been out to Vegas in July. He had been there a half-dozen times altogether, and this was his third trip to the Mirage Casino since they started the drug-store jobs in the spring of 1994. The best was last year, when he had come out after robbing an illegal casino in Ottawa. The place was usually open 24 hours a day, but the guy who ran it closed the place down once a year for cleaning. Kevin broke the lock on the door, snuck in past the cleaners and grabbed $45,000-worth of chips before anyone knew what was going on. He was in and out in less than 90 seconds. The next day, before the chips were noticed missing, he and some friends came in and took turns cashing in the hot chips. After paying off his buddies, Kevin had $35,000 in cash in his pocket and he caught the next flight to Vegas. The money lasted four days. He'd even been up more than $200,000 at one point, but a bad run on the blackjack table left him with nothing but his return ticket home. Kevin had been out to Vegas enough times now that he was getting to be quite well known there.

Tyler returned from checking out the lobby. He was playing it tough; he had been out to Vegas once before with Kevin. But for Yves, this was his first time.

A red-vested bellhop had their luggage and led them into one of the gilded elevators. He pressed the penthouse button. They didn't say a word until the bellhop, with a new $100 bill in his pocket, left them alone in the three-bedroom suite overlooking the burning lights of Las Vegas.

Then it was Tyler's turn to smile. This was the life.

They took quick showers and then changed into fresh clothes: a Ralph Lauren blazer for Tyler, a Hilfiger shirt and some khakis for

Yves. Kevin went for the Hugo Boss with his sports pager tucked into the inside pocket.

"You think they're treating us well now," mused Kevin as they were in the elevator going down to the casino floor, "wait until we buy our chips."

They went to the back of the casino to the blackjack tables where the minimum bet was $500 a hand. Kevin pulled out $20,000 U.S. and asked for chips. Yves followed cashing $20,000 and Tyler asked for $15,000 in chips.

Within seconds, there were three waiters at their side, loading them up with double ryes on the rocks. A slick manager in an Armani suit slid up to them to personally welcome them to the Mirage.

They were going to play some cards.

September 14, 1995
Ottawa, Ontario

Tyler pulled on his bathrobe and went to answer the door. Who the hell would be pounding like that at 3 a.m.? He opened up the door. And got a gun in his face.

"The money. We want the money, motherfucker!"

There were two of them, each with a balaclava to hide his face. They slammed the door behind them and forced Tyler to the floor.

"We want the money. Where is it?"

Tyler wasn't going to mess around. Not with guns. "Under the bed. The red Nike box. Take it, just fucking take it."

One of the men ran to the bedroom while the other kept his gun on Tyler.

This was the second time he'd been robbed. Everyone in the gang was starting to get hassled. They had been just throwing around too much money. Word had been getting out and now they were easy targets. Tyler reminded himself to get another apartment.

"Got it!" The second man emerged from the bedroom with the shoebox and they both left.

Tyler was left face down on his apartment floor, $18,000 poorer. What was he going to do? Call the police?

Fuck.

CHAPTER FIVE

October 28, 1995.
Ottawa, Ontario.

Yves downed his rye in one gulp and waved over to the bartender for two more. Kevin had his head buried in his hands.

This was crazy.

Tom Glavine had pitched excellent ball, shutting out the Cleveland Indians, and David Justice had pounded a solo homer for the game's only run. The Atlanta Braves had just beaten the Indians 1-0 and won the World Series four games to two. This was very bad.

Already down $15,000, after losing $3,000 on each of the first five games, both of them went double or nothing on Game Six. Their luck, the worst ever, had to change. The Indians were sure to win. Now they each owed $30,000.

Yves downed his fresh drink. Kevin still hadn't taken his face out of his hands. So Yves drained his drink too.

"We are the two unluckiest men alive." Yves ordered two more rye and cokes.

Their World Series debacle was hard on the tail of the Vegas fiasco. Yves had dropped $30,000 U.S. there. Kevin had been up $75,000 after three days, but blew it all and $15,000 of his own money on day four. They were haemorrhaging money.

Seventeen months on the job and several million dollars later, it had come to this: they were both completely broke.

"I guess we're going to have to work hard next week buddy," Yves mumbled.

Kevin slapped him on the back. Fuck Las Vegas. Fuck Atlanta. They'd get it back.

November 8, 1995
Winnipeg, Manitoba

Marc raised his gun and crept forward. He had turned off the light on his mining helmet so he would have the advantage of surprise. Yves was standing between the household goods aisles six and seven, setting up an ambush with empty laundry hampers. He was a sitting duck.

He crept closer. Closer. Now.

"You're dead, motherfucker."

Yves spun around. Marc pulled the trigger. The Nerf rocket bounced straight off Yves's forehead and he dropped to the ground. Marc unslung his Super Soaker water rifle and pumped a round into him. Yves screamed as the ice water soaked his crotch.

Marc turned and ran. Hit-and-run. That was always the best approach. He skidded around the corner of the aisle and headed for the safety of the men's clothing section.

That sound. He stopped. What was it? It sounded like tires on the tile floor. And it was . . . behind him! He turned. He was staring straight into the lights of Kevin's mining helmet. The bastard had scammed a bicycle from the sporting goods section and was coming at him full bore. Holy shit. And he was holding a sponge mop like a lance.

Marc turned and started to run, but before he got five feet, the soft head of the mop pounded into his back. He lost his balance and went rolling into a display of Turtle car wax. The hard plastic bottles cascaded over him.

When he dug himself out, was staring right into the barrel of Kevin's Super Soaker. He dropped his weapons and raised his arms. He was defeated.

So he checked his watch. Whoa. "Kev, its 3:30 a.m. Let's get the safe and jet."

Kevin checked his own watch. Play time was over. He saw Yves sneaking up behind Marc with an armload of women's' bras. "Put 'em down Yves. We've got to work."

Yves scowled and dropped the bras.

They had arrived in Winnipeg the previous day, having bought last-minute tickets at the Toronto airport. Ontario was getting stale. They had been working it for 18 months and had hit close to 120 stores successfully. If you counted the other 80 or so where they had blown the alarms early or where there was shit-all in the safe, it meant they had hit every ripe job in the province. There were hardly any good scores — single-story stores in deserted sections of town — left to hit. They wanted some virgin territory.

So far, the airline tickets were paying off. This Walmart had zero protection. They had some motion detectors but the dumbass who had put up the Sale! signs had incredibly blocked them all. The beam couldn't be broken. There could have been 10,000 people in the store and the alarms wouldn't have gone off. Total idiots.

They found the safe and popped it. $30,000.

November 15, 1995
Calgary, Alberta

Marc was babbling. "Consulting, man, consulting, there's a lot of money in it."

Kevin and Marc had dropped a couple grams of mushrooms each, and were wandering the streets of deserted downtown Calgary. It was warm and windy — an unusually early chinook was coming through.

"I'm telling you," Marc said, his voice racing, hardly breathing, while Kevin walked silently, taking it in. "I incorporate myself, print up cards and the like, break out one of my suits, get a briefcase, maybe some of those fakeass glasses, for the professional look. Then go around to stores with high robbery rates. Tell 'em I'm a specialist, and for a premium fee, I'll ensure they never get robbed again."

"You'll guarantee this?" Kevin asked, .

"Yeah, hell fucking yeah. 'Marc Flamini Consulting. Never Again.' That'll be the slogan: 'Never Again.'"

"And what will you say your qualifications are?" Kevin asked smiling. "Almost two years of drug-store and other robberies? You can knock out motion detectors in seconds? Or perhaps your high school diploma . . . wait, you don't have one."

Marc looked at Kevin. Asshole. But it was true, his plan seemed to have a major flaw. "We're never going to live a straight life are we?"

"No," Kevin said. "But at least we're going to live forever." And at 3 a.m. in Calgary, Alberta, mid-November though it was 5°F, they were.

November 21, 1995
Miami, Florida

Kevin had paid $1,200 to the scalper for the seats, but they were worth it. Right at field level, between the 40- and 45-yard line. He could practically smell Dan Marino's sweat.

The game between the Miami Dolphins and the San Francisco 49ers was at halftime, so Kevin let himself melt into the humid Florida night and leaned back with his beer. The 49ers were pounding the Dolphins and the big Monday night game was turning into a fiasco. But what did Kevin care? Besides, with one more touchdown, Marino would break yet another record. This was too sweet to complain about.

He looked over at Linda, a University of Miami student he had met last night at a bar. He had been so impressed, he even took her to the game and bought her a ticket. Now she smiled at him, her short, brown hair tucked into a Dolphins cap and her beautiful eyes sparkling.

To think, just three days ago he had been in Calgary.

The gang had just pulled a jerky little score on a Pharma Plus. There was a lousy $18,000 in the safe, hardly worth their time. They had gone back to the hotel after, rolled some joints and watched the late-night telecast of SportsDesk on TSN.

It had been such a shitty little score, sitting there on the table, looking sad and pathetic.

Yves grabbed a deck and made a proposal. “We all draw cards. High card keeps it all.”

They were stoned and bummed out at the score. They all agreed.

Kevin drew first.

A jack of diamonds. Fuck. It was high, but no way would it last.

Marc drew next.

Six of hearts. Burnt.

Yves drew.

Ten of hearts.

“Sorry Yves,” Kevin said, laughing at his luck. Asshole thought he’d take the haul home for himself.

Kevin looked at Tyler. He drew.

A deuce.

Kevin’s take had just quadrupled. It was time to treat himself.

Next morning he caught a flight to Miami. He had even offered to buy tickets for the other guys but they had refused. They wanted to do another score and get some money. Kevin had a flight booked up to Victoria for the next morning. He would rejoin the guys and finish whatever work they had set up, then head back to Ottawa.

Kevin finished his beer and tucked the plastic Dolphins mug into his bag as a souvenir.

The second half was about to start.

November 22, 1995
Saanich, British Columbia

The guys were famished.

It was four o'clock in the afternoon and they hadn't eaten all day. They had left Calgary early the previous morning, after four easy scores and $110,000 more in their pockets. On the last one, a Safeway grocery store, they had tripped an alarm on their way out and the alarm bells had been thundering. The guys figured that was a sign. Calgary had been good to them, so why push their luck?

They had spent yesterday afternoon scoping a Shoppers Drug Mart, met Kevin's flight and then spent the night downing rye and smoking weed in their hotel room. They had been planning to go out to a bar and try to pick up some women, but they figured, why bother? They flipped through the Yellow Pages and ordered in.

They woke just after 2 p.m., hungover and hungry. They took turns in the shower and ordered a pizza. They were going to work tonight, so they needed the food. Yves was cleaning up when the pizza arrived. He was looking under his bed for his wallet, but instead found the condom he had used last night with his call girl — Samantha? It was still sticky and wet. He tossed it at Kevin.

"Fuck you Yves. I'm eating."

Tyler was in the shower, so Marc, Kevin and Yves tried to finish off the pizza before he came out, just to piss him off.

There was one piece left when Marc stopped them.

"Wait. Tyler should have at least one piece. Besides, I have an idea."

As soon as they shouted that the pizza had arrived, Tyler jumped out of the shower. "You fuckers, where's the rest?" he shouted, stuffing the piece into his mouth.

He stopped. Reached up to his chin.

The condom was hanging out of his mouth.

Tyler's eyes went wide. Everybody scattered. "Motherfucking douchebags."

November 23, 1995
Saanich, British Columbia

First the condom, then this.

Tyler slammed open the door to the police station and walked out onto the street. Marc was still inside, signing the last of his release papers. The fucking cops had nailed him and Marc for the job at the Shoppers last night. The fuckers.

Yves and Kevin were waiting out on the street, having had to come down and get them after the arrests. Fortunately, they were released on their own recognizance.

This sucked.

"How'd they get you?" It was Yves, looking a little bit cocky.

Tyler shrugged, and swore again, but Marc had just stepped out of the station and began explaining how the cops had taken them down. "Someone got suspicious when we were scoping the store yesterday afternoon. A jerkass manager jotted down our license-plate number after we left. When they got hit, they remembered the plate and tracked it straight to the hotel. While you guys were out getting Kentucky Fried, the cops came and scooped us up. The bastards."

Yves blinked. He had wondered why the hotel room was empty when they got back with the chicken. Tyler and Marc had gone to the Shoppers alone to check out the interior before doing the score. One of them must have gotten sloppy and tipped off store security, who followed them out to their car after they left the store. It must have been pretty simple for the cops to track them down after that. Two suspicious characters in the store during the day and it gets robbed at night. All they had to do was track down the rental plate the guard had given them.

The four of them got into the car, all of them silent. There was nothing worse than taking a pinch.

"Don't worry too much," said Kevin. "They can't have anything solid."

Tyler nodded. There was no evidence, no prints in the store, nothing. But the case would be a hassle. They were going to take the ferry over to Vancouver tonight and figure out what to do. It depended on how stupid the cops were. Marc and Tyler had given the police a Victoria address so they wouldn't connect them to the jobs back home.

This could screw up the whole operation if it got back to Ontario.

They would have to think, and think hard.

November 29, 1995
Vancouver, British Columbia

Yves and Tyler didn't even breathe.

They had decided to be lazy, and instead of going through the roof of the drug store, they'd snuck into the stockroom and hid behind one of the enormous stacks of boxes. All they'd do is wait until the staff went home, walk up to the manager's office, pop the safe and they'd be gone. Who cared if they set off the alarm on the way out? Their rental car was right out front. They would disappear into the late-night haze of Vancouver traffic in seconds.

They had been leery about doing one last job after Marc and Tyler got pinched in Saanich, but they wanted some money to take back to Ontario. They figured they'd be in and out quick, then hop the plane in the morning.

Now this.

"All right, Tyler," said Yves. "If they come for us, stick your hand down the front of your pants. Start screaming like crazy, telling them you have a gun. I'll do the same, right?" Tyler nodded.

The store had closed at 9 p.m., just like it was supposed to. They had heard the announcements over the PA system. They figured they'd be ready to go in an hour. Instead, it was like rush hour.

There must have been 20 stock clerks in the back room, unloading boxes, stocking shelves. Yves and Tyler were shitting themselves. They had been lazy and were paying the price.

Tyler checked his watch.

It was 3 a.m. The clerks had been at it for more than five hours. Sooner or later they were going to get to the boxes the guys were hiding behind. Yves and Tyler could hear them right close, cracking open boxes of Comet and Mr. Clean. This was going to be ugly.

Another hour passed. They could hear every word the clerks were saying. They were only a couple of feet away.

Then: "That's the last of them, boys. Let's pack her up."

What?

They heard shuffling and laughing, and then the lights went out. Yves and Tyler looked at each other. What the fuck was going on? They stood up, and stepped out from behind the boxes. Their bones ached.

The back room was empty. When they had hidden, piles of boxes were everywhere, towering up to the 20-foot ceiling. Now they were all gone. Except for theirs.

They turned around.

Scrawled in heavy, black marker across the three dozen boxes they had used for cover were the words, "For Shipment to Victoria."

Dumb luck.

"We shouldn't press it man," urged Yves. "Let's jet. It's 3 a.m." All of a sudden he really hated British Columbia. Two disasters in less than a week. Yves was getting real homesick, real quick.

But Tyler crept to the swing doors that opened up onto the store floor. He turned back to Yves with a mischievous smile. "Fuck. Let's do the job anyway. We have an hour."

Yves thought about it for a second. He shrugged. Why not?

December 14, 1995
Ottawa, Ontario

Yves screamed as he brought the pick down hard on the roof of the K-Mart.

"*Yesss*. I should write a fucking book!"

Smash. The pick came down hard again.

They had been talking about diversification for the past few weeks, ever since they got back from British Columbia. They had agreed to keep on working, to wait and see how things turned out in B.C. for Marc and Tyler. There was no way the police here would connect the Saanich incident to the Ontario crimes.

But where to hit? They had scoped out almost every major drug store in Ontario and hit every one they could. Some of them twice. They had been all over – Ottawa, Kingston, London, Sudbury, North Bay, Peterborough — fuck, every major city in Ontario. There was getting to be slim pickings.

The only place they hadn't hit was downtown Toronto. They weren't stupid. There was too much heat there. Bars and sophisticated alarms on all the stores, heavy-duty cops. Fuck that. They didn't need that shit.

So they wanted to go into other businesses. Open up new markets. Yves had been watching the news and had seen a piece on the new videogame machine from Nintendo. It was super-hot, every kid wanted it – hell, almost every kid had one already. The game consoles were cheap pieces of shit, and only sold for $200. The real money was in the cartridges that sold for between $60 and $80 each, said the reporter on television. Sixty to eighty bucks a piece for those small things, thought Yves. Hey.

They had hit an Electronic Boutique outlet in Belleville the previous week and had walked away with more than a thousand game cartridges. They had sold them through Woloski for $30 a pop. You couldn't scoff at a $30,000 score.

They had scoped out the games department of the K-Mart yesterday. By their count there were more than 2,500 cartridges there, what with the store stocking up for the big Christmas shopping rush. Hell, there must have been five hundred copies each of the new Mario Brothers and Donkey Kong cartridges, the best-selling ones on the market.

That would mean a score of $75,000. Great fucking money. Sure, it would be a pain in the ass to drag 2,500 cartridges out of the store. They were forced to steal a pickup truck for the occasion. But you couldn't beat the money.

Marc and Kevin cleared away the tin and insulation. Yves peered down the hole.

It was a 15-foot drop, so he lowered himself through, hung from his hands, then let himself go. Kevin and Marc followed. The cartridges were stored behind sheets of plexi-glass with pathetic sliding locks keeping them closed. Kevin went through, popping the glass open with a crowbar while Marc and Yves followed, sweeping the cartridges into heavy, industrial-strength garbage bags. In 30 minutes, they had filled seven bags.

They pulled them all to the back door, disabled the alarm and waved Tyler over.

Who said Christmas shopping wasn't fun?

December 31, 1995
Acapulco, Mexico

Kevin and Tyler could barely keep from looking at the women strolling down the beach. It was like a Miss America contest. And they'd brought their girlfriends. Damn.

The four had figured, what the hell, why not treat them? The girls deserved it. It had seemed like a good idea at the time. Now they were all hanging out on the beach, having a bit of fun. But no Miss America for tonight.

Kevin stood up and headed for the water. What the hell. It'd been a good year. A great year. The best of his fucking life. Sure, the money situation wasn't the best right now. Despite all they'd managed to earn, Kevin was down with the bookies. But there'd be plenty more coming their way. One thing for sure, this trip would buy enough good will from Sylvie for another couple of months of bingeing.

Kevin stared out at the choppy Pacific Ocean and the clouds that were drifting on the horizon. Maybe tomorrow, they'd rent a boat and do some deep-sea fishing.

He could go on like this forever.

Chapter SIX

October 1995
Kingston, Ontario

Det. Const. Mike Fagan knocked on the glass door, leaning his head into his partner's office at the Kingston headquarters of the Ontario Provincial Police. "Hey, Bow. You're not going to believe this. That was the Waterloo force on the phone. We could have another half-dozen cases on our hands. They're going to go through the incident reports again and get us the files by the end of the week."

Det. Staff Sgt. Glen Bowmaster arched his thick eyebrows and leaned back in his chair. Holy shit.

He scratched his black mustache and peered over at the stack of manila files that was already teetering on his desk. How many stores had these guys done? It was getting ridiculous. He thumbed through the stack of reports. There were bingos, Dairy Queens, Beaver Lumbers, more drug stores than he ever knew existed — Big Vs, Pharma Plus's and what seemed like a never-ending stream of Shoppers Drug Marts. Bowmaster had seen a lot of crazy cases in his 30 years with the OPP; hell, they were all pretty crazy. But he had a gnawing sensation in the back of his mind: This one could top them all.

"All right, Mike. Looks like we're going to be claiming a little more OT."

Fagan nodded, and cracked a smile. As if we'll get it, he thought to himself as he left Bowmaster's office. He had about 60 days of time-off owing to him as it was because of the overtime he'd put in. Bowmaster was in the same ballpark. This investigation would add another couple of dozen days to the total. The thing was, neither of them would ever see the time-off. If you took a three-month fishing trip, you were out of the game and you fell behind on your cases. There was no time for holidays, not when there were so many little ratfuckers out there Fagan wanted to nail.

"Just what I need, more OT, Bow. I'll get back to you if I get something else," Fagan shouted over his shoulder as he headed back to his desk.

Bowmaster nodded absent-mindedly to his partner, stretched his arms and then stood up so he could look out the window. It was the middle of October 1995, but the summer had been a good one and now the warm weather was stretching right into the fall. From his window, Bowmaster could see the hills sloping down to the St. Lawrence River, the trees starting to become a brilliant splash of orange and red as their leaves turned for the winter. On the street below, a group of young women, most likely Queen's University students, paraded by still dressed in light, summery clothes. Bowmaster spotted one of them in a tight jean skirt and let out a low whistle before catching himself. "That could be my daughter," he mumbled, still sneaking one last look at her bronzed calves.

This was as spectacular a fall as he could recall. You could still sit out on the back deck, barbecue some ribs and down a couple of cold Molson Exports most nights. Bowmaster turned from the window and looked back at the pile of files on his desk. If this case even got anywhere near the size it was promising to . . . well, he might as well forget about enjoying the fall weather.

The case had erupted several weeks back, on the Labour Day weekend, when that stupid punk Colin Freeze was caught trying to squirm his way into the back room of a Mac's Milk in Kingston. The clerk had seen his ass sticking out of the fridge and pressed the silent panic alarm. Luckily, officers were on patrol just a couple of blocks away and when they arrived, Freeze was in the back room, shoving cartons of cigarettes into a garbage bag. The police took the kid — he was only 17 — back to the Kingston station, and prepared charges of trespassing and break-and-enter.

They had been in the questioning room all of five minutes when all of sudden Freeze, a thin, blond kid with a serious case of nerves, started talking. The punk must have thought he was on some kind of American TV show where he could get the charges dropped for information. Freeze had babbled on for 45 minutes naming every jaywalker, dope-smoker and shoplifter he had ever known. It was all garbage. The investigating officers booked him for break-and-enter anyway.

But one thing had stuck out. The kid said he knew some real big-time guys in Ottawa, the same ones who had bragged about how easy it was to do the convenience-store cigarette jobs and told him how to pull them off. According to Freeze, who had sweat rolling down his forehead from his mess of blond curly hair, these guys were involved in all kinds of crimes. But their specialty was some kind of rooftop entry jobs on supermarkets or drug stores. Freeze said the gang had done hundreds.

It seemed bogus, like everything else Freeze said, but Kingston had had a couple of stores hit exactly the way he described so it struck a chord with the officers. It just so happened that one of Bowmaster's colleagues, Sgt. John Peterson, had been assigned to investigate those crimes. To be safe, the officer took down two names from the kid — Kevin Grandmaison and Yves Belanger — and passed the information and interview notes on to some of the department's senior investigative officers, who passed them on to Peterson.

You never knew what might happen. Peterson had been on the case for a couple of months, but a couple of break-ins hadn't been that big of a priority and he hadn't invested much time in it yet. Maybe this was a break.

Of course the way the police bureaucracy worked, the same week the Freeze kid got booked, Peterson got reassigned. His cases got spread throughout the department. It was a pain in the ass for the Kingston office, already short-staffed. No one needed extra work and most complained bitterly, including Bowmaster.

The complaints fell on deaf ears. The break-and-enters fell in Bowmaster's lap. He had gotten the file in the first week of October and let it sit on his desk for seven days of silent protest. Bowmaster was already behind on a couple of cases, and when he spent a dinner break reading Peterson's case file, he wasn't even sure what to do with the information. He had checked the file on the Freeze kid: a record the length of your arm, all petty crimes and misdemeanours, but a real sleazebag nonetheless. He was the kind of kid who'd connect his own mother to the Paul Bernardo case if it would save him a couple of days in jail.

The tips about Grandmaison and Belanger were most likely crap, figured Bowmaster. But what the hell. There had been grumbling around the department about the number of break-ins recently, so it would be good to get a major bust — the gamble could be worth it. All it would cost him was time. He already put in about 70 hours week, what were two or three more?

The first thing Bowmaster did was pull the files on reported rooftop break-and-enters in their jurisdiction — the greater Kingston area. That was his first surprise.

Everyone at the OPP station in Kingston knew there had been one or two rooftop jobs recently. It was an unusual crime and they stood out. But according to the files, it wasn't just a couple. In the past 15 months there had been reports of seven such break-ins in the area. That was goddamn serious. Bowmaster wondered why no one had picked up on the trend before.

Bowmaster then went back over the notes of the Freeze kid babbling. He mentioned *hundreds* of cases. The number sent shivers up his spine. All of a sudden, maybe this didn't seem like such crap anymore.

Bowmaster went to his department supervisor and asked for some time and some help. He had a hunch this could be big, and the department had learned to trust Bowmaster's hunches. He called up his longtime friend and partner, Mike Fagan, who was working out of an OPP office in Ottawa. Was he interested in a couple of days on a break-and-enter case? It could get real interesting, promised Bowmaster. Fagan, also in tune with Bowmaster's hunches, couldn't resist an offer like that and drove to Kingston the same day.

The newly re-united duo tracked down Freeze at a Vanier apartment where he was spending his time smoking hash and frequenting strip clubs alone while he waited for his court date. The guy was living like a rat, and while Bowmaster and Fagan were there, he fried up six eggs just so he could suck the yolk out of them. Fagan thought he was going to vomit when he saw that. Still, Bowmaster and Fagan spent three hours peppering him with questions. For nothing. The Freeze kid knew shit.

He had only heard rumours of the rooftop jobs and had offered it up in desperation, hoping he might be able to swing a deal or get some sympathy for being such a good guy. Freeze seemed shocked that the cops were taking it seriously.

But he must have been tight with them, said Bowmaster. Hadn't they taught him the convenience-store job?

Freeze looked embarrassed. He had a friend who knew Grandmaison and Belanger and told him the rough details of how it was done, explained Freeze. Obviously they hadn't told him enough or he wouldn't have been caught. But that was it. He had never even met Grandmaison or Belanger.

Who was the friend?

Jake . . . something. Freeze couldn't remember his last name.

Convenient. Bowmaster asked the question again, this time letting the kid know his break-and-enter case would go a hell of a lot worse if he didn't start co-operating.

Freeze collapsed, and broke down in tears. It was a complete dead end, and Bowmaster and Fagan left.

With Freeze a waste of time, the next obvious step was a background check on the two names they had: Kevin Grandmaison and Yves Belanger. Fagan ran the names through the Canadian Police Information Centre, the system that tracked every arrest, police charge and conviction in Canada. Neither Grandmaison or Belanger were angels. Although they had never been convicted of anything, there was a steady line of little items, times charges had been dropped or the guys got unconditional discharges or warnings from the judge: possession of narcotics, possession of stolen property, some theft under $5,000, but it was all from when the two were young offenders, and that information could never be run in court. More interesting was a charge they had faced together for breaking into a bingo in 1993.

According to CPIC, the case had been thrown out of court, so Bowmaster called some Ottawa cops for the buzz. The word was that police had tracked Grandmaison and Belanger after a smash-and-grab at a bingo. It was pretty easy, it had been winter and all the police had to do was follow the footprints in snow to a Nepean apartment. But all the evidence they had was circumstantial. No prints, no witnesses, and despite a two-hour search of the apartment, no stolen merchandise. According to the Ottawa cops, there was no doubt the two were guilty, just the evidence was weak. The best thing they had was some glass fragments in the bottom of their shoes that matched the bingo's broken front window. It was tight, and the cops figured that might have been enough for a conviction. Until the glass-fragment expert failed to show in court, having decided to give birth the day Grandmaison and Belanger were due to appear. The case collapsed without her and the charges were dropped, letting the two walk.

Still, it made Freeze's story more plausible. No priors for rooftops, but at least it looked like they had the potential.

In any case like that, the fingerprints were kept in the system just for good measure. Bowmaster and Fagan thought they might get lucky and match some prints from the scene of one of the Kingston rooftop jobs to Grandmaison and Belanger. They went through the old files, but they didn't make a single match. Not one print had been recovered from any of the crime scenes.

No prints, no reliable witnesses. All of a sudden, Bowmaster's hunch wasn't looking so good. With two strikes against them, Bowmaster and Fagan put out a bulletin to police agencies across the province asking for any reports of similar incidents: break-ins at drug stores or other single-story businesses where the thieves went in through the roof and popped the safe.

Home run. Within a week they had heard from three other forces and the count was up to 16. After two more weeks they were at 39 and with the Waterloo police, it was 45. And there were still more forces to hear from in Ontario. It was unbelievable. Even Bowmaster was surprised. He thought he might find 20 jobs, tops.

The total was staggering and the magnitude of the crimes was even more staggering. From the 45 break-and-enters that had been reported so far, the losses were reported at close to $2 million. In each case, the same things went missing: cash, stamps, lottery tickets, traveller's cheques and money orders. The drug counters were never touched, which was unusual. The drugs in a standard pharmacy could be turned over for twenty or thirty thousand on the street, so they were a hot item. It was all too much to be a coincidence. Everything pointed to it being the work of the same people.

There was even better news. They had talked to the Durham regional police, based east of Toronto. They reported five rooftop break-ins, but even more important, they had a detective who had a special interest in the case.

It seemed there was an attempted break-and-enter at the Pier One Imports store on Stephanson Road in Oshawa on February 18, 1995. Someone had gone in through the roof, and a safe inside the store was moved to the rear of the building and then just left there. The thieves apparently got spooked by something. It just so happened the sister of one of the detectives who took a report on the Pier One case worked at a motel in nearby Whitby, the Comfort Inn. The detective and his sister talked the next night, and the sister mentioned four men dressed in black sneaking back into the hotel just after 2 a.m.

"Just thought it was suspicious and you might want to know," she told her brother.

The guys the sister had seen left in a hurry the next day, so there was no chance at asking some questions, but the detective took the pertinent information from the room. It was registered to one Kevin Grandmaison. The Durham detective hadn't gotten any further than that, but would it help?

Bowmaster could have kissed him. He finally had some kind of corroboration for Freeze's story. It was incredible. They had a raft of cases and now some good suspects. Bowmaster rubbed his sinuses. It was coming together like Lego, but it was going to be a headache.

Kingston's experience had been repeated across the province. Police forces thought they were dealing with one or two of these rooftop jobs, but when they started going through the files, there were two or three times that. However, there were so many different police jurisdictions in the province and whoever was committing these crimes roamed so freely through each of them, there were never more than seven or eight break-and-enters with one force. That was one of the reasons the individual police forces had never been overly alarmed, and one of the reasons why Bowmaster had such a big headache.

There were just too many jurisdictions involved. Too many officers to organize, too many files to retrieve, too many budgets that were too tight to provide funding for the investigation.That meant the OPP would have to carry the ball and co-ordinate the entire investigation. As the only agency that has the stature and powers to work with all the different forces in Ontario, it would be their show.

It was going to take thousands of hours of police time which meant upwards of a million dollars. The OPP was the only force with that kind of budget and it looked like they were willing to spend it.

The head of Bowmaster's unit was Detective Insp. Pat O'Brien. As soon as the first reports came in from across the province, tipping them off about the potential size of the case, Bowmaster and Fagan went to O'Brien.

Even though he had left the crime work and gone up to administration, O'Brien hadn't forgotten what it was like to be on the street and how important it was to have the right resources to fight the war. So many times in the past, O'Brien had come through for Bowmaster when he was needed, and this time looked like it wouldn't be any different. After getting a briefing on the case, O'Brien got the devil-in-the-eyes look, the one he reserved for the lowest of the low. He turned to his officers and pointed at them.

"Do whatever it takes, understand me? I want these guys off the street. This is a priority."

When O'Brien gave an order like that, you knew it was serious. He was a take-charge cop and a great boss. Fagan and Bowmaster knew they were going to live and breathe this case.

In the two weeks since then, it had been Bowmaster and Fagan's life. Their wives liked to joke that the two of them should be married to each other they were spending so much time together. It was just the beginning.

After getting the responses from across Ontario, Fagan and Bowmaster decided to push their luck and put out a bulletin to break-and-enter squads from across Canada. Although it could take weeks, even months for details to come back from other provinces, considering how quickly this operation was growing, Bowmaster wouldn't be the slightest bit surprised if they got some cases from across the country.

This case was starting to roll. Bowmaster took another look outside at the splendid fall weather. There was always next year.

At least he and Fagan had names: Kevin Grandmaison and Yves Belanger. Suspect one and suspect two.

Bowmaster took a sip from a glass of water that stood on his desk, smiled, and put the glass down.

It was a start.

Bowmaster and Fagan looked like cops and they liked it that way. They were both big men with the ruddy complexions of outdoorsmen and thick mustaches covering their upper lips. Bowmaster's hair was shoe-polish black, but Fagan's went gray long ago. Considering Fagan had just celebrated his 50th birthday in the last six months and Bowmaster was coming up fast on the same milestone, they were in good shape. The detective work that took up most of their time meant they didn't get in many physical confrontations anymore, but they could still kick the ass of men half their age.

Teamed up on the rooftop case, they looked like brothers working the case and talked like it too, taking jabs at each other's weight, grooming habits and taste in clothes. Their jovial nature together helped them get through the sometimes intense boredom of page after page of information and data.

Bowmaster had worked with the OPP for almost three decades, joining the force in 1967 when he was just 21 years old. In those days, all you needed was a high school diploma, a strong body and a smart mind. Bowmaster was perfectly suited for the job.

He started out doing the beat work in small towns, breaking up bar fights, chasing stolen cars. He moved to Belleville after a couple of years on the force and was put on criminal investigations. Bowmaster had found a home.

It was in 1975 that Bowmaster had first teamed up with another young cop, Mike Fagan, for an OPP investigation in Kingston. Fagan had joined in 1969 and had also been working in Belleville on criminal investigations. He was a year older than Bowmaster and the same hard-nosed kind of cop. He'd once worked 67 straight days, many of them 18 hours long, helping to take down a hash ring. He'd do anything to complete an investigation, and that attitude quickly endeared him to OPP administration.

It seemed like a perfect match when they were teamed up for the job in Kingston in 1975. As they worked on the rooftop case, in fact, they couldn't help but draw parallels between the two investigations. Their first case together was remarkably similar to the one they were teamed up on 20 years later. There had been a string of break-ins in the Kingston area, where guys had gone in and cleaned out offices. A hydro office had been hit, a Zellers, a bunch of hardware stores and even a little mom & pop grocery store.

The modus operandi was the same for all the jobs. In through the back door using lock cutters or crowbars to get through the door and then loot the office. In those days, small stores had no alarms and the locks were still pretty basic. They were easy picking. Fagan and Bowmaster were on the case for three weeks, shaking down every small-time hood and drunk driver they could arrest until they finally got a tip. A group of friends headed by two brothers named Cousineau had been doing the jobs. They were all in their early 20s and had previous records for drugs and stolen cars.

After a two-week stakeout, Bowmaster and Fagan caught the boys in the act, breaking into an insurance broker's office, looting it for about $500 cash and a truck-load of office equipment. The Cousineaus and their friends ended up going down for 13 jobs in all, with the total stolen coming in at a bit less than $50,000. It was good, quick police work and got the young cops noticed.

Soon they were getting teamed up on a regular basis, handling murders, narcotics trafficking and biker gangs. As the duo entered the twilight of their careers, their resumés even contained such big-name cases as the infamous investigation into St. Joseph's Training School in Alfred, Ontario, halfway between Ottawa and Hawkesbury. Allegations of sexual torture and abuse at a church-run halfway home led to one of Canada's largest sexual-abuse scandals. With the help of Bowmaster and Fagan, the OPP made arrests that led to the conviction of 16 church officials.

After all those years together, the two had started spending their time together away from work too. Whether it was a weekend at a cabin or four days down south for some fishing, they were almost inseparable.

And now, two decades after they first worked the Cousineau case together, they were back to break-and-enters. The modus operandi was different and the criminals were a bit more clever this time, but in Bowmaster and Fagan's eyes, it was no different. They were still a bunch of punks destined to see the inside of a jail cell.

Y Y Y

Bowmaster looked around the table at the roughly 30 men who had arrived for the meeting. It was an impressive crew.

There was himself and Fagan, along with a couple of other OPP officers and teams from the Ottawa-Carleton regional police, the Orillia police, the Chatham police, the Durham regional police, the Halton regional police and the Waterloo regional police. There were also representatives from Canada Post, Pharma Plus Drugs and Shoppers Drug Mart, who had a definite interest in these break-ins being stopped.

They had all driven down to Kitchener, Ontario, for this October 28 meeting called by Bowmaster and Fagan. They had to put a plan together because Bowmaster and Fagan were getting pissed. Real pissed.

In the past two weeks, since Bowmaster and Fagan had received permission from O'Brien to tackle the rooftop gang in earnest, things had been going very slow. It was painstaking, frustrating work trying to co-ordinate so many officers and consolidate so many different reports. Hell, it had taken a week just to set up today's meeting alone.

Meanwhile, the men responsible for these jobs were working overtime. There had been eight fresh reports of rooftop break-ins since Labour Day. Shoppers Drug Marts in Pickering, Hamilton, Oakville, Mississauga, London, Strathroy and St. Thomas all had been hit, all for considerable money. The last report was of a place called The Gallery in Brantford. These guys had been criss-crossing the province, stealing at will. And it made Bowmaster furious.

But the past two weeks had turned up some good things. After a little surveillance work, the Ottawa-Carleton police also had no problem identifying who might be doing the jobs with Grandmaison and Belanger. Every two-bit hood in the city knew of the four pretty boys who drove fast cars and flashed fast cash. The three nights Ottawa-Carleton had them under surveillance, these four guys had been out on the town, each night with different women. That gave Bowmaster and Fagan two more names: Marc Flamini and Tyler Wilson.

They had also compiled an overall list of jobs done in the province that matched the description. By the end, it was stunning. There were about 140 cases in all, carried out in 21 different police jurisdictions. Fifty of them were just attempts, where alarms were triggered and stores reported damage to their roof, or the roof was reported as the attempted point-of-entry. That left 90 successful jobs. Of those, another 50 were super clean. No prints, no alarms, no leads. It was the last 40 that piqued Bowmaster's interest. These weren't quite so clean. There were snippets of videotape, prints, in one case human feces. Things they could go on. Things they could nail these guys with. Follow the smell of shit and you'll find the shit bag responsible.

They spent eight hours in the meeting. Each force gave brief summaries of the rooftop jobs in their jurisdictions along with a list of what evidence they had. It was meagre. No, it was goddamn pathetic.

There were in-store videotapes, but few had any good face shots. In one, the thieves had plastic shopping bags over their heads, in another they wore balaclavas.

The best tape they had was from a Shoppers Drug Mart in Chatham. The store had motion detectors three feet off the ground, so the thieves were sliding along the floor. Two men went through on their bellies. The final one went through on his back, clutching a money bag against his stomach. The face was blurry, but Bowmaster was pretty sure they could match it to Grandmaison. But of course, pretty sure wasn't enough.

They wanted to take these guys down hard. To do that, they needed to connect them to a string of jobs, prove to a judge these were hardened criminals maliciously seeking out and destroying businesses. Even more tantalizing, these guys could lead them to who *knew* what other corruption. They weren't just taking cash, they were taking stamps and lottery tickets. You needed a distribution system for that. Hell, if the cops played this right, they could fill dozens of cells.

There was no question what course to take. First, O'Brien summarized the investigation again, making sure the Ottawa-Carleton police were ready to take part. With the gang based in Ottawa, the investigation would need a lot of help and resources from the Ottawa cops. O'Brien looked over at Staff Sgt. Lance Valcour, who was the senior Ottawa-Carleton officer at the meeting. "You can spin these guys for us?"

Valcour nodded. "We could have tails on them tomorrow if you want. We're with this 100 per cent."

O'Brien smiled and then gave the floor to Bowmaster before the meeting broke up. "We'll take this in three phases. First surveillance. We'll watch these punks, get a feeling for where they're going, what they're doing, who their friends are. Maybe get first-hand proof of a job. Second, once we get enough evidence together, we'll take it to a judge and get some phone taps on these characters. Maybe wire up their apartments too.

"Once we get proof of activities and connect the guys to their hood friends, we'll move in. That'll be the third step, taking them down on the job. We don't want any circumstantial evidence here. We want the hard stuff. We want to catch them in the act, OK?"

The men around the room nodded.

Bowmaster spoke one last time. "I think we can have this thing in place within 30 days."

Thirty days. It would be tight, thought Bowmaster. They still had to get a team together, set up a headquarters, arrange a budget, make sure there was financing in place. And of course, they'd need a name for the investigation.

"How about Fiddler?" suggested one of the officers.

Huh?

"You know, like the musical there, *Fiddler on the Roof*?"

Bowmaster smiled. He liked it immediately.

Project Fiddler was born.

Y Y Y

Bowmaster took a gulp of his beer and leaned back in his chair.

He couldn't believe his initial optimism. Thirty days. It must have been the lingering warmth of the Indian summer that made him naively optimistic. It had been 90 days and things still weren't off the ground. He looked outside at the flurries of snow that were pounding against the window of the bar. Yes, late January in Ottawa. What a fine time of the year.

A plump waitress was busy taking down Budweiser football signs and decorations. It was the Monday after the Super Bowl and the bar was still recovering from the drunken rowdiness that goes with the big game. The Cowboys had beat the Steelers by two touchdowns, but at least Pittsburgh had kept it close late in the game. It was the best Super Bowl Bowmaster had seen in a while. Now he just wanted a quiet drink and wished the waitress would stop ripping down the decorations.

It had been one hell of a day. After weeks of working on the investigation's organization, getting background on Grandmaison, Belanger, Flamini and Wilson, and a million other bureaucratic hassles, it looked like the project was set to roll. They had just finished everything they would need to get an authorization to intercept private communications from a judge. They had put Grandmaison, Belanger, Flamini and Wilson on the application along with Sylvie Guttadauria, Grandmaison's wife. They expected the wire taps to be in place by the first of February.

Mere days, Bowmaster thought. Time's almost up, and this time he was serious.

The plan was simple. To keep tabs on everything said, wait until the gang hatched another plan to go out (as they inevitably would, figured Bowmaster), follow them out onto the job and take them down. They had an agreement with every force in Ontario. If the gang went through their jurisdiction, the force would free up officers for a spin team to follow the gang. Everyone was also briefed to make sure the guys weren't taken down unless Bowmaster and Fagan knew about it first. He didn't want some cops in a place like Timmins, who had zero knowledge of the case, stumbling onto the gang and wasting the questioning period with useless questions.

The delays were a problem though. It seemed every week they waited another business got hit. It was now January 29. Since the October 28 meeting, there had been another 11 reports of jobs in Ontario. It was frustrating. It was insanely frustrating. You knew it was going to happen, you knew how it was going to happen, you just didn't know when and where.

Bowmaster felt like going to Ottawa, dropping in on Grandmaison, tipping his hat to Sylvie, and punching the fucker out right there in his living room, fast car parked on the street. But he was a man of procedure. This operation was going to go right. That was simply that. As soon as the phone taps were in, they'd know the score. The police would watch the gang do a job, and Bowmaster'd greet them afterwards at the hotel: "Hello boys, it seems you're under arrest." These four young men would pay.

Bowmaster fingered through the four best shots of the guys from the surveillance work done by the Ottawa-Carleton cops. Lately, he was carrying files from the case everywhere he went. They were omnipresent, the case was always on his mind. Kevin Grandmaison, Yves Belanger, Marc Flamini and Tyler Wilson became little ghosts that spun around his head 24/7.

Grandmaison stood a little under 6 feet. His head was squarish round, a hint of a square jaw, but it was simply solid. Grandmaison had some serious bulk, from years of weight lifting. His lips, usually kept tight together, made it seem like he was scowling. Hair, a little longer on top, short on the sides. Dark brown, like everyone in the gang, except Wilson.

Wilson's hair was light brown, almost blond. He had a preppy hairstyle, parted in the middle, falling evenly on both sides, but the side and back of his head were kept short. He was usually smiling, with a nice tan.

They were all handsome kids, but Marc Flamini was the looker in the group. Round, smooth features, dark eyes, a deep tan like the rest of them.

Belanger had a stronger face, his curly hair trimmed short and eyes always darting. A square jaw, like someone chiselled his face from a stone, and his body even harder. Belanger was stacked.

Bowmaster stared at the colour glossies. With the beer in him, the shots didn't seem real. Each photo, each guy, they were all fresh-faced, clean-shaven, young. They were dressed up like they had just finished a photo shoot for *GQ*. Instead, they spent their time going through the roofs of businesses. It was a crazy world. Damn, how did these four kids get here? Fuck, Bowmaster thought. A long string of robberies with millions stolen, almost countless people and businesses screwed over by these assholes, that's how.

But it was going to come to a screeching halt. And when the four made it in front of a judge, the party would be over. Over for a long time, Bowmaster hoped. And in spite of all the delays, the case moved forward, baby step by baby step. Little gems even trickled in one by one. And the best one was brand new. The break of a lifetime came in today.

The Canada-wide bulletin Fagan and he had put out in October had already resulted in some calls, all from British Columbia and Alberta. Bowmaster had thought it looked like the work of the same gang. As of this morning he knew it was.

He'd gotten a call from the Saanich police. It seems they had made an arrest on November 23, two men. A Tyler Wilson and a Marc Flamini.

The Shoppers Drug Mart had been robbed there for a substantial chunk of money. Rooftop entry, safe cracked, exact same modus operandi that Bowmaster had read about in a hundred police reports. It was a clean job. The Saanich police had no clues, no leads. They thought it was going to be unsolved.

Then a stock clerk spoke up. Something weird had happened the day the store was robbed. He had gone into the back room to get a case of Tylenol — the store's shelves were empty — and ran into this tall, blond guy staring at the roof and checking out the manager's office.

The guy had claimed to be looking for the bathroom, but the clerk was suspicious. He followed him out of the store, and had even jotted down the license plate of the car the guy was driving. Did the police want it?

It was a break all right. The plate was a rental car from Hertz, so it wasn't hard to guess that their suspects were from out of town. They checked the hotels and on the third try they found the car at the Red Lion Motor Inn. They asked the hotel clerk to call up to the room and ask the persons inside to move the car.

Ten minutes later, Tyler and Marc were in the lot. Arrests were quickly made. There was no solid evidence, so the two were released on a promise to appear before court the next week. The police had asked that they be kept in custody, but the judge had a soft heart. The two young men were both clean-cut, well-spoken and neither had a criminal record. And they also lied. Flamini and Wilson gave the judge an address in Victoria, said they lived there. That swung it for the judge. If they were local boys, no way would he hold them.

Saanich was Fedexing a copy of the case file down to Kingston. Poor bastards. The cops out there had a better chance of winning the 6/49 than seeing those boys in court. But it was certainly going to make the case against those pricks stronger when Bowmaster got them into court.

He finished the rest of his beer and prepared to head out into the snow. Fagan was back at the office, finishing up the paper work for the judge so they could get the wire taps.

Bowmaster needed a rest and was going home to his wife to spend the next day with her. He figured once the taps were in place, he wouldn't sleep until he got what he wanted: The pleasure of seeing those pricks behind bars.

Chapter SEVEN

February 14, 1996
St. Catharines, Ontario

"Come on boys, do it for us. That's it. Climb the roof you little bastards."

Const. Mike Haslett was sitting in a blue Taurus, one of the force's fleet of undercover cars. He was watching the Shoppers Drug Mart on Glenridge Avenue through his binoculars and had just seen the suspects' car, a red 1996 Pontiac Sunbird with license plate 636 YHB, pull into the parking lot and disappear down a back street behind the Shoppers. According to the computer, it came from E-Car rentals in Ottawa, rented by one Jennifer Hayes. In the briefing Bowmaster had given over the radio, he had told them that Hayes was an ex-girlfriend of one of the four suspects, Marc Flamini. Real nice, thought Haslett, getting your girls involved like that. This Hayes woman would be thrilled when she found out what the car was being used for. Haslett shook his head without realizing it and continued to stare through the binoculars. The Sunbird zipped around the rear of the drug store and disappeared.

It was show time.

Haslett, a wiry officer whose uniform always seemed about five sizes too big, was on the stakeout with Const. Mark MacKinnon. The radio that sat between them in the car had been erupting every 30 seconds, giving updates on the Sunbird as it left the Howard Johnson and sped around town. The boys seemed to be driving randomly, probably trying to determine if they were being followed. They probably figured since there were no cars on the street, they were clear.

Yeah, right. There was no way in the world the department would be that obvious. Bowmaster and Fagan, the guys who masterminded Project Fiddler, had made sure there were lookouts stationed around town so they wouldn't have the problem of glaringly obvious tails following the gang. It was pretty easy to keep track of a car after midnight in St. Catharines. The streets just weren't that busy.

Haslett and MacKinnon had been shadowing the guys, on and off, for the past two weeks. They were part of a 12-person spin team, officers assigned to monitor and record the gang's actions. It had started in Ottawa, keeping track of who the guys hung around with, where they ate, what they spent. After a week, Haslett even knew how many squares of toilet paper the punks used when taking a shit. They had been that close.

But then there was that fuck-up. Major fuck-up. The guys had given them the slip on February 9th, a Friday. There was a team following Grandmaison, who was driving his wife's white Suzuki Sidekick, and a team following Belanger, who was driving a red Accord. That Friday afternoon, both Belanger and Grandmaison had met at the Hard Rock Cafe in the Market. The tails, accustomed to the gang's many lunches and dinners out, had decided to stay outside and watch the vehicles. After two hours and growing suspicion, one of the officers went inside to check out the restaurant. No sign of Grandmaison and Belanger. Half an hour later, Sylvie Guttadauria wandered into the parking lot and drove away in the Suzuki. The Accord was left parked in front of the Hard Rock. They had been given the slip. There was no sign of any of them — Grandmaison, Belanger, Flamini or Wilson — in the days following. Haslett was happy he wasn't on duty when the gang got away. Bowmaster and Fagan weren't pleased, and shit had hit the fan.

But Haslett had to hand it to the gang. The guys were good to give them the slip and get away with what they were doing. They had to be good *and* smart, or their break-and-enter scheme wouldn't have gone this far. Haslett hadn't believed it when he read their profiles. Suspects in at least 100 jobs, with estimates going as high as 250 in total. These punks had each stolen more in four years than he would make in his entire career. It made him angry. It made him passionate. It was wrong, and he was going to help right it.

It took the police a couple of days to track down the four of them again. The reports of an attempted break-in in Orillia told them that the gang was on the road in the Toronto area, ready and eager to work. Then police had intercepted some calls made from a phone booth in Brantford on February 12th. They were able to get a spin team from the Brantford police force down there within minutes, who followed them until the Project Fiddler team could take over. From there, it was simple surveillance. Well, not quite simple. The way these guys drove, 150 kilometres an hour everywhere, it was tough to keep a tail on them and remain inconspicuous. Still, they managed to track them to the St. Catharines hotel. Now the police were ready.

Haslett lit a Camel and sucked back a lung-full of smoke. Tonight they were going to take down these preppy little bastards. "Okay, come on boys. Let's do a little digging, shall we? That's it. You think we can't see you. We see you, you little fucks."

MacKinnon looked over at his partner with disdain. "All right, all right, enough with the goddamn play-by-play," MacKinnon said, wanting his partner to just shut up.

MacKinnon was sitting in the passenger seat of the Taurus and pounding back an extra large Tim Horton's coffee. It was his fourth of the night. He hated these long stakeouts, all the hours in the car, his legs falling asleep, his back aching. It was a pain in the ass. He had been with the OPP for 11 years and he still got stuck with these lousy assignments. And his partner's exuberance was beginning to irritate him. Haslett was only a year removed from police college and still got excited pulling over speeders. If the guy ever had a serious case, a murder or a hostage-taking, he'd cream himself. Haslett reminded MacKinnon of those over-eager, security-guard types who always wanted to get their man. He watched as Haslett continued to scan the roof with the binoculars. Hell, he was probably going to cream himself tonight if this thing went down.

MacKinnon grabbed the radio and made a call back to headquarters to update Bowmaster and Fagan. "Yeah, it's MacKinnon here. The suspects have arrived on the scene and are on the roof. We have everything under control. We'll call back when there's movement."

The radio crackled with interference. Then came Bowmaster's raspy voice. "They didn't see you, did they?"

MacKinnon and Haslett exchanged glances. No chance of that. They had been parked behind a Bank of Nova Scotia building when the Sunbird pulled in, totally out of sight. Now they had moved again to get a better view and were parked safely behind a gas station. No way would they have been spotted. "Negative."

MacKinnon turned the radio off and took another swig of coffee. Putting the coffee down, he finished the last of his cigarette, tossing it in the ashtray quickly filling with his and Haslett's butts. The two continued to monitor the gang's progress. They couldn't see much up on the roof, but there was only one way out of the parking lot. As soon as they saw the Sunbird pull out, they would head back to the Howard Johnson and get them in the room. Bowmaster and Fagan wanted them after the job was done, in the hotel room to prove consistent practice and premeditation. He also hoped they'd recover some of the scores the guys might have made on their road trip.

Haslett put down the binoculars and rubbed his eyes. According to reports, it took the guys anywhere between one and three hours for a job. Most of the time they cracked the safe inside the store, but there were some reports of the whole safe being taken. So far, 45 minutes had passed and there had been little movement.

"Hey. What's that?" Haslett saw some shadows moving on the roof. He fumbled to focus his binoculars in on the movement. He saw somebody standing near the edge of the roof, then disappearing out of his line of sight. It was probably the watch. Or less likely, maybe the job was done. They would have to stay alert.

Two men appeared on the roof. One stared straight at their Taurus, making a slight motion towards it. The men talked, standing close together. One started walking around the perimeter of the roof, and then they both disappeared.

"What's going on?" Haslett said, voice racing. "What's going on? Maybe we should radio back in."

"No. Wait. Wait and see what goes on," MacKinnon answered.

Haslett kept the binoculars on the roof. Then the distant sound of an engine. That was the Sunbird. Twenty seconds later it roared out from behind the drug store. He turned to MacKinnon. "They must've seen us."

"It doesn't matter now, let's go," MacKinnon said, as he pitched his coffee out the window. "The job's over fast, that's all." The faster the better on a night like this, he thought. It'd be nice to be home early.

"OK boys," Haslett said, getting excited. "Looks like you're in for a little surprise." Haslett kicked the car into drive and sped off for the hotel.

Y Y Y

"What the fuck?"

MacKinnon and Haslett were in a room at the Howard Johnson overlooking the hotel's parking lot that had been reserved by the force earlier that night. The curtains were drawn, but MacKinnon had the binoculars pushed through a crack and was watching the Sunbird pull into the parking lot. They had beaten the guys back to the hotel, but that wasn't a surprise. According to the intelligence reports, they always drove around town after, making sure there was no tail and sometimes stopping for food, drink or women. Or all three.

Haslett and MacKinnon had already made sure the hotel's manager knew what was going down and had done a quick walk-through of the place to make sure nothing was out of the ordinary. The last thing they needed was a drunken trucker beating on a prostitute in his room or some road-weary family from Calgary pulling in as late-night guests when the bust was about to go down. But everything was quiet, and other than the low buzz and blue light of a couple of televisions, all the rooms were dark.

Still, as Grandmaison, Flamini and Wilson left the car and headed for the Howard Johnson, MacKinnon thought there was something strange about the situation. The guys weren't carrying anything. No money bags, no nothing.

That didn't make sense. No alarm had gone off at the drug store. Bowmaster had called to tell them he assumed it was a sign that the guys had successfully busted the safe and made the score.

But now no bags. Maybe it was in the trunk. Wait, there was Belanger. Did he have something in his hand? MacKinnon couldn't tell. Even more strange, they were no longer dressed in the black clothes they'd seen them in earlier. He leaned over to his partner. "When they were on the roof, they were in black, right?"

Haslett nodded and looked equally confused. Now they were dressed in nice shirts and jeans or khakis, looking for all the world like a bunch of preppy students from Brock University after a night out on the town. Strange.

"What the fuck?" MacKinnon sat up. Grandmaison had stopped dead. He was talking to the other guys. Shit. They were heading back to the Sunbird. Then out of the corner of his eye, he saw Belanger. He focused the binoculars and tried to get a make on him. Nothing. Wait. There he was now, heading back to the car. No bag, no nothing. MacKinnon couldn't believe his eyes.

What the hell was going on? It was almost as if they had felt the heat, as if they recognized their Taurus in the parking lot or something. But that was impossible, wasn't it? Now they were all getting back into the Sunbird. This was bad. MacKinnon elbowed Haslett. "Call headquarters. They're getting out of here, we need the cavalry."

Haslett called Bowmaster. Bowmaster flipped, the stress of what was supposed to be the climax of the investigation collapsing on him.

"We wanted them in the room!" Bowmaster shouted over the radio. Calming down, he continued, "Shit. We needed them in the room."

"Look, I don't know what's going on," replied Haslett, flustered. "Do you want us to move? I'll go." He reached for his gun, tucked into a leather holster on his belt.

Bowmaster was cursing into the radio. "Fuck it. Stay where you are. Make sure nobody from the other rooms comes out. And make the fuck sure no employees come out wanting to be heroes. Got it? We're taking them in the parking lot. We don't need anything else. We have enough to make the case against them."

The radio went dead. There were a dozen squad cars, plus the tactical and canine units staking out the hotel. It was time to move in.

The cruisers came soaring over the crest of the hill and down into the parking lot. The guys in the Sunbird didn't even bother trying to get away. They opened the doors of their car and leaned against it, waiting for the inevitable. MacKinnon, peering through his binoculars, saw four faces: anguish, anger, sadness and a blank stare.

MacKinnon and Haslett shared a grin. Things may not have gone according to plan, but the end result was still the same.

They were going down.

Y Y Y

The cops didn't use kid gloves.

One shoved Marc hard against the car hood. Kevin and Tyler were roughly searched and then pushed into the back seat of a cruiser. Yves had his arms twisted high against his back before he and Marc were put into a second police car. Next destination: the holding cells of the St. Catharines police station.

On the ride to the station, Kevin just stared out the window, watching the street lights and store fronts, everything so bright and vivid it hurt his eyes.

For the past 10 years he had been preparing himself for a moment like this. When he had first started doing break-and-enters, back when he was just 15 years old, he worked with a guy named Derrick Pilon. Derrick was a good guy to work with, he knew a lot stunts because his dad was a bit hood, having done a couple of stints for armed robberies. One of the garbage clichés Derrick always used was if you do the crime, be prepared to do the time.

Kevin hadn't seen Derrick for years, but he had taken that to heart. He was no kid and he wasn't going to break just because they had been pinched now. He was ready to pay the price. But it was hard. When he and Yves had been nabbed for that bingo, it didn't seem real. It didn't mean anything to him and he got off so easy, it was quickly forgotten. Now, hell, he was married. Married for two years. He'd known the joyride would end, but he figured it would be his own decision to pull out. He didn't appreciate these fuckhead cops making the decision for him.

Kevin looked over to where Tyler sat. There was a vacant look on Tyler's face, but his eyes were blinking that nervous blink of his. It was Tyler who was so cautious back when they started up with Woloski in . . . holy shit, that was May 1994, almost two years ago. Had the rooftop jobs been going on that long? The time had flown, just flown. Tyler had been right then. They should have been more careful. But he was just as guilty as anyone else now. They had all been caught up in the thrill of it: the women, the travel, the money, the gambling. Now they were paying the price. The question was, figured Kevin, was the ride worth the price of the ticket?

They made eye contact. Kevin winked at Tyler and he cracked a grin.

"This is nothing, these pricks are nothing," Tyler said, his cockiness returning. Kevin laughed.

The two rode the rest of the way to the station in silence. The same couldn't be said for Marc and Yves.

"You prick. Can you say police brutality? Can you fucking spell police brutality? I can spell it. B-R-U-T-A . . . are you getting this? I can slow down. L-I-T-Y. I want your badge number and your name you piece of shit." Marc had been yapping at the cop driving the car for 10 minutes. His shoulder was sore from where he had been jammed into the hood and his shirt was ripped. He could not wait to talk to a lawyer.

"Are you the same cocksuckers who let Bernardo run wild?" It was Yves now, cracking wise about Paul Bernardo, the St. Catharines man who had gone on a rape and abduction spree under the noses of local police that had left three teenage girls dead. "Good work. Real smooth guys. You guys must have been top of the class, eh? You St. Catharines cops must be some real beauts."

The cop driving didn't even turn around, content in knowing that this night, he would be sleeping in his own bed. The assholes in the back seat would be trying to curl up on a cold steel cot. That would cool their tongues.

When they arrived at the station, the four were taken from the cars and led into the dingy police station in downtown St. Catharines, and put through the process.

After being fingerprinted, photographed and strip-searched, the group were lead into the dank, gray cell-block. They might as well have been aliens for how much they stuck out.

There were a dozen cells, all carved into a single concrete wall in the basement of the police station. Seven of the cells were filled with exactly the kind of men you'd expect to find there: a pathetic wino, draped in dirty rags with a twisted beard full of burrs; a long-haired freak with tattoos of big-breasted women and demonic spiders running up and down his forearms; a huge man with a goatee and a black Harley Davidson T-shirt stretched across his enormous belly; and four other low-lifes you'd cross the street to avoid. It was a motley crew.

And into that mess walked Kevin, Yves, Tyler and Marc. Four pretty boys with trendy haircuts, luxurious tans and expensive clothes. They looked like they should be teeing off for a round of golf at Pebble Beach, not preparing to spend the night in the decrepit St. Catharines jail.

As they walked past the other inmates, the usual din of the cell block fell silent. Who the fuck did these guys think they were, prancing in here like that?

It was the man with the tattooed forearms who spoke first. "What the fuck do we have here? Eh, you rich bitches? Are these the little shits from 90210?"

Yves winced when he heard that. His girlfriend loved *Beverly Hills 90210*, an evening soap opera that followed the lives of some rich, good-looking pretentious pricks whose parents had more money than Bill Gates. Needless to say, Yves hated the fucking show.

The guard behind them chuckled. "That's a good one. 90210 — it's like we nabbed 'em from some champagne reception. Some fucking *champagne* gang."

"Fuck you prick," Yves spat at the guard, missing far left.

They passed another cell, where a tall man with deep-set eyes was pressing his face against the bars. He smiled at Kevin. Then spat at his feet.

Kevin lunged at him, stopping his fist just before the bars. They weren't going to fuck with him.

An officer grabbed him and shoved him further along the corridor. The man with the deep-set eyes glowered at Kevin. "I like your shirt, asshole."

The four were put two to a cell at the end of the corridor with the three empty cells separating them from the other prisoners. As the door shut hard on Marc and Yves's cell, an officer smiled at them. "Get used to it."

Marc sat down hard on the steel bench. It was cold and the cell stunk like urine. He grabbed his hair in his hands and pulled, hoping the jolt of pain would clear his mind. He hated those prick cops. He hated being under their control. Why hadn't he quit after Saanich? His instincts had been screaming at him. But they were making so much money, the scores were so easy . . . it had all been such a good time. Shit. He knew he should have quit.

He thought of his girlfriend, Terri Anne. It was so fucked. She would be pissed. No, she'd be more than pissed. Oh, fuck, it was basically over with her if he went to jail. He winced. She still didn't know anything about this and, of course, he hadn't told her about Saanich. That seemed so little league. This was the majors. This wasn't some cops getting lucky and holding no evidence. This was a squadron of cops tracking them back to their hotel after a job, this was Yves's uncle's warning, this was probably phone taps. He was starting to panic. He would definitely tell Terri Anne about this. He would have to call her.

What would he say? "Hey, Terri. Happy Valentine's Day again. We got a little off track down here. Arrested and all. We'll be home in a couple days." Marc sunk back in his own depression.

Yves was talking through the bars to Kevin and Tyler. Marc could just hear snippets. They wanted to make sure everyone knew how to handle the situation.

Yves turned and looked at Marc. "You solid?"

He knew what Yves was asking. Was he going to admit anything to the cops? Was he going to tell the cops about their history? Was he going to try and cut a deal? Was he a fucking idiot? "Give me some goddamn credit. Of course I'm solid." He was solid. He'd tell the fucking cops where to put it. Yves came to the bench and sat down beside Marc. They waited. And waited. And waited.

Hours must have passed with them just staring at the flaking, damp walls of the holdings cells. Finally.

"Kevin Grandmaison." It was said in a toneless voice, like attendance was being taken in elementary school.

"Kevin Grandmaison." The repeated words roused Marc from a light doze. There was some kind of banging sound. Where the fuck was he?

He opened his eyes. Oh yes. Jail. He must have fallen asleep. What time was it? It must almost be morning. He looked up. There was some fat cop in a uniform banging on Kevin and Tyler's cell. "Kevin Grandmaison, get the fuck out of there."

Kevin appeared, rubbing his eyes. He must have drifted too.

Marc nudged Yves awake and they talked for another few minutes before falling back asleep. They were awakened when Kevin was returned to his cell and Tyler was taken up to the questioning room.

Yves and Marc pressed up to the corner of the cell to get the word from Kevin.

"They want to know all kinds of shit. They want to know why we did the store, where the money is, they want us to give them the hotel key. Fuck, they keep on talking crazy shit."

"What'd you do?"

"I told them to fuck off, just kept on denying everything. I asked for a lawyer."

"What case do they have?"

"They say they know everything, but I think that's shit. I don't know." Kevin sat back and wondered. Maybe they did know everything. That was a fucking shitload of cops for an isolated hit. They had to know of at least more than one job to justify the force they brought out to bring them down. And the blue Taurus. Undercover surveillance. Shit, this was bad. They could know everything, and if that was the case, it was over. It could be over for a long, long time. This was really fucking bad.

They waited another hour and Tyler returned to the cell block. He went through the same questioning and denied everything. Marc was next.

He entered the room and there were two cops, a thin guy in a suit with a goatee and police ID around his neck. Sitting beside him was an older guy, balding with glasses and a sickly pale complexion. The one with the goatee offered him a Player's, which he gladly accepted and let the cop light it for him.

"Hi Marc, my name's Grant Ellis. I'm a sergeant with the OPP. Doing all right?"

Marc nodded.

"Make it easy on yourself, Marc," Ellis started, sliding the lighter back into his shirt pocket. He was tall, over six feet, red hair, blazing red goatee, his voice stern yet yielding, a strange calming influence. "Just tell us what happened and get it over with."

"Fuck you."

"Look, why are doing this?" Ellis smiled at Marc, who seemed to be staying strong. "You're still young, don't try to act tough. Let's work this out."

"Fuck you," Marc repeated again. "I want a lawyer."

"Look son, your friends have already co-operated. They've told us how you planned the job, how you came from Ottawa just to hit this store. Give us your side of the story."

Marc coughed up some smoke and started laughing. "You guys are fucking ridiculous. You're a joke. You're trying to convince me the boys ratted us out? That they talked? No. You're both fucking jokes. Get a real job."

Ellis shrugged, sat down, and lit himself a cigarette. The bald cop stood up, identified himself as Const. Pat Bateman, and leaned over Marc. Here it goes, thought Marc, the tough cop. Who were they trying to kid?

"You know, the hit we busted you for is going to land you in jail. Why don't you start talking, you little shit."

Marc just stared back at Bateman all glassy eyed.

"Listen you little motherfucker," Bateman said in a low growl, the words burning the back of his throat before spitting them in Marc's face. "We watched you go into that Shoppers. We watched you come out. We have you by the balls and I'm going to enjoy tearing them off. You ever done time? You will now, cocksucker. Now tell us what happened. Now." Bateman leaned forward, his nose almost touching Marc's nose. Marc held his ground, staring, quiet, sincere, almost earnest, as though this had been a small misunderstanding.

"Well, sir. Me and my friends are on our way to the casino in Windsor, but we got tired and stopped here. We thought we'd go out to a bar and get some drinks to wind down. We did. We came back to the hotel and you were there. It's your mistake."

Bateman pulled back and slammed his large fist down on the table, rattling the legs, the boom echoed through the entire room. He turned, paced, picked up a chair, slammed it down too, and then turned and faced Marc from halfway across the room.

"You're pretty, you know that," the words rang in the small interrogation room. "You know what happens to pretty little boys like you on the inside? You're going to be someone's bitch Marc. Some big bastard is going to enjoy pumping your ass in the pen. And you know what? I'd like to see that."

"Fuck you," Marc shrugged.

It went on like that for another half-hour, Ellis getting Marc coffee and cigarettes, Bateman ranting and raving. Finally, they let up and Marc was returned to his cell.

He slumped down on the bench while the guards led Yves upstairs for his questioning. He'd done good. Those cops didn't have anything. Marc wondered if they had found the garbage bag with the black clothes and rubber gloves. That could screw them. He hoped Yves had hidden it well.

"So?" It was Tyler, his voice coming from the next cell.

"They think we're a bunch of kids who are going to fucking roll over and cry," Marc said. "Fuck them. They don't know shit about us. We're solid. We're not going to break."

Tyler nodded. "A-fucking-men."

"Nothing was taken?"

Bowmaster was thundering around the cramped administration offices of the St. Catharines police station. It was 7 a.m. on Valentine's Day, four hours since they'd brought the gang in. The Niagara police hadn't laid any charges yet, they hadn't even talked to any of them yet. The gang was just cooling their heels in the holding cell until Bowmaster and Fagan came up with a plan of action.

So far, only the local St. Catharines police officers had shown their faces to Grandmaison, Belanger, Flamini and Wilson.

And it would be the St. Catharines team who would do the interrogation. Bowmaster and Fagan didn't want to make an appearance, they didn't want to tip their hands that they were onto the whole scheme. He didn't want those kids to know just how close Project Fiddler was to bringing them down.

"Damn," Bowmaster swore again, the other officers in the room exchanging nervous glances. The charges against Grandmaison, Belanger, Flamini and Wilson were being prepared, with the police hoping to nail them each with one count of break-and-enter with intent and one count of conspiracy to commit break-and-enter for the Shoppers.

Intent. Bowmaster had wanted the real thing, not intent.

First, before the charges, there was the questioning. The plan was to just nail them with questions about the one job, hint at others, but to grill them on the St. Catharines Shoppers and hope the gang broke.

If they miraculously admitted to doing the whole string of robberies, bonus. If not, book them on the single set of charges and release the four of them. Then it would be a simple matter of seeing where they go and building the rest of the case.

Y Y Y

Bowmaster and Fagan sat and drank coffee for the next five hours, listening incredulously as the questioning took place. The four of them were hard, no doubt about that. Despite the grilling, no one offered anything useful. No one said a thing that was useful.

After it was over and the boys back in their cells, the two cops doing the questioning, Ellis and Bateman, came in and poured themselves coffee.

"Nothing we can use," shrugged Bateman. "Let's get the charges laid and let them have their lawyers."

There was nothing left to be done. Bowmaster and Fagan gathered their files and prepared for the drive back to Kingston. Once the charges were laid, the four would be held in custody until they had a remand hearing. That would be one or two days depending on the court schedule. Then, considering they had no priors, the judge would release them with a promise to appear back in court on a later date. There was nothing else for Bowmaster and Fagan to do.

Well, one last thing. Bowmaster looked up at Ellis. "Make sure that you ask the Crown to get non-association as part of their bail. It'd be good to get some breaches."

Ellis nodded. That was like asking to make sure Christmas fell on the 25th of December. It was standard procedure for the Crown to ask that while co-accused were before the courts, they not be in each other's company. When the four were released from jail, they would sign the standard release form agreeing to that condition. What Bowmaster was betting was that these four would have trouble staying away from each other. Hell, they practically saw each other every day. When he and Fagan were ready to take them down for good, they could cite every time they broke their bail agreement as a sign of disrespect for the law. These breaches made people look bad.

"Go home and get some sleep, Glen. You and Mike Fagan

deserve it. We'll babysit these kids for a couple of days, then they'll be yours again. Don't worry."

Leaning against an aging window frame, Bowmaster let the early morning light fall across his face. He smiled. It hadn't gone picture perfect, but they had got enough. He wasn't worried.

Y Y Y

Terri Anne, Tania and Sylvie were waiting on the steps outside the St. Catharines police station, clutching their jackets against their bodies to shield against a stiff wind.

They had driven down from Ottawa, leaving early on the Monday morning. They had got the calls from jail on Wednesday, Valentine's Day. It wasn't the present they had wanted.

Kevin, Yves, Marc and Tyler had spent five days in jail, waiting for their remand hearing on Monday morning. As expected, they were released on their own recognizance, with various conditions, including non-association, curfews and an order not to be within 1,000 metres of a drug store after 6 p.m. and before 10 a.m. Inside, the last of the paperwork was being filled out before the four could be released. It would be a long drive home.

Kevin and Yves got off pretty easy paying $750 each for bail. Marc and Tyler got nailed for double the amount each, $1,500, because of the bust in Saanich.

"What an ugly city." It was Sylvie, trying to make some small talk. She felt bad for Tania and Terri Anne. This had come as a huge shock for both of them. They hadn't even guessed what their boyfriends had been up to. Kevin at last had let Sylvie know a little bit of what was going on. Late last year, on their first anniversary in Jamaica, he laid it out. He had just said his past wasn't as clean as he wanted it to be and he still had a few problems he was trying to clear up. It didn't take much to figure out from there that all the money Kevin was spending wasn't acquired completely honestly.

Sylvie was about to try another stab at conversation when the door to the station opened. They were out, left with nothing but the clothes they had been wearing when they were busted. The rental car, and all their things from the hotel room, had all been seized as evidence.

Marc had lipped off to the cops about that. How the hell were they supposed to get home? It was a joke.

They exchanged hugs with the girls and then split up into two cars for what would be a lousy winter day. Seven hours back to Ottawa. Yves, Kevin, Tania and Sylvie took one car while Tyler, Marc and Terri Anne took the second. But before they hit the road, there would have to be one stop. The first thing they had to do was go see if that bag was still there.

It was Marc and Tyler who drove over while the rest drank coffee at a downtown diner. The place looked different during the day. The parking lot of the Howard Johnson was practically empty at 1 p.m. on a cold Monday afternoon. A light snow had fallen, and the place looked serene and innocent. Nothing like the eerie night sky lit up by the squad of cop cars and their bright blue and red flashing lights when the gang was busted. It was hard to believe it was the same place. It was like stepping outside your body and looking at yourself — the exact same, but the perspective, time or space, made it look strange and surreal.

Marc pulled the car into the lot and stopped at a parking spot farthest from the manager's office. No way did he want to be seen around here again. It was embarrassing. But more important, if the cops caught them here, they could find the bag. And if they found the bag, they would find enough evidence to scorch them for sure.

Marc did a quick check around the lot. It looked quiet enough. "Okay, Willy, who's going to go in and look? You or me?"

Tyler wasn't having any part of it. "I'm staying here. Fuck this. I've been through enough."

Marc shrugged. Yves had given him exact instructions on where to find the bag. It should be no problem. "Fuck it. I'll go."

He stepped out of the car and headed around the back of the hotel, going in through the rear door. It was after checkout time and before anyone would consider checking in, too much daylight left to drive in. The place was a tomb. He walked through the first floor corridors until he found the door to the staircase. Down one flight to the basement.

It was there.

"Je-sus Ch-ri-st," whistled Marc. "This can't be true."

He jogged up three flights of stairs to see if anyone was lurking. Nobody. He headed back down and grabbed the bag.

Everything was still inside.

He headed to the car, flipped his hair back, and raised the bag over his head triumphantly. "It looks like luck is finally on our side."

Once they were outside of St. Catharines city limits, they stopped at a McDonald's. Marc and Terri Anne went in and ordered up a load of Big Macs and milkshakes while Tyler tucked the garbage back into the McDonald's Dumpster. They made small talk while they ate, knowing full well that they had just dodged a bullet. But they were still staring down the barrel of a pretty big gun.

At least now they were going home.

Chapter EIGHT

February 1996
Ottawa, Ontario

Yves sat and stared glumly at the plate of blackened catfish and Cajun-fried vegetables that sat in front of him. He and Tania were sitting together at Big Daddy's Crab Shack and Oyster Bar, a trendy new restaurant that had opened up on Elgin Street in Ottawa. It was Yves and Tania's first real time alone since the St. Catharines fiasco and so far the evening had been, well, awkward. He had promised he would take her out and explain everything, explain the endless weekend trips away with the boys, explain all the money he was bringing home, explain the crime. Now that it was actually happening it was too painful for both of them.

"We didn't hurt anybody, Tania. I swear. Everything we did, anybody we hit, it was covered by insurance. There were no guns, nothing like that." Yves stopped and scanned the room for their waitress, a blond hardbody with a great tan and short black shorts. His glass was empty, long empty, and his body was demanding more rye to cope with the stress. Finally, the blond appeared from the kitchen with a tray of appetizers and Yves caught her eye and raised his empty tumbler.

"Look, I love you," continued Yves. "I never wanted to hurt you or anyone else, that's why I didn't tell you. It just got so out of control. Trust me, after this, I'll never go back." He stared at her, trying to make some eye contact, but Tania just sipped her glass of wine and pushed some pan-fried shrimp around on her plate.

"Yves, I don't know what to say. Of course I still love you, but I'm hurt. And what's your family going to say? They'll have to know and after all they've been through . . . ." Tania's voice trailed off and she looked up at Yves now, her eyes sad and on the verge of tears. Yves's heart was being torn apart.

The waitress arrived with the much-needed rye and coke, which Yves accepted with a nod. He took a long pull, grateful for the distraction.

Tania was right. He would have to tell his mom. And that would be truly hard.

He had always tried to help out his mom, Noella Belanger, with a bit of money here and there, telling her it was from work or gambling. She was such a good woman, a strong woman, who had done so much for him as a child. She had raised Yves and his twin sister Yvette by herself, making do on the money she made as a nanny and from babysitting. They had lived early on in the Ritchie Street projects, one of the worst areas in Ottawa. Somehow, some way, she had scraped together enough money for a down payment on a plot of land on Haughton Street in Britannia. Not the wealthiest area in the city, but a world of difference from Ritchie Street, with good schools and safe parks for the kids to play in. For two years, Noella dragged Yves and Yvette to the land every weekend, helping dig the foundation, spread gravel, move beams — anything to save money as they built the house. When Noella had money, the construction went on. When she didn't have money, the construction stopped.

When the family finally moved in, it was like the start of a new life. Sure, there still wasn't much money, but they owned their home and everything was different.

It was one of the reasons Yves felt like such a shit when he started out doing small jobs. His mom had lived hard all her life, but she had done it honestly. Yves just couldn't resist the money that was available to young men willing to compromise their ethics, and he couldn't miss the chance to give a little bit back to his family.

"Yves, how's your mom going to handle this?" Tania started up again, breaking the minutes of silence. "After everything in the last year, your dad . . .," her voice trailed off, the words collapsed on themselves.

He pushed away his catfish, having only had one bite. His stomach was in a knot and he couldn't stand the guilt. Tania was right. Breaking the news of the St. Catharines bust would be even harder on his mom considering what the family had gone through last year.

Noella had always told the children their father had died when they were young, and Yves and his sister always took her word for it. But out of the blue last year, a man Yves had always known as a friend of the family had come forward and insisted on talking to Yves and Yvette. He was their uncle.

Noella had once dated a man when she was very young, but the relationship ended and the two went their separate ways. Almost 10 years later, the man was married and had a family, but was having troubles at home. He moved out of the house and after a couple of months started dating Noella again. It was a short, but passionate fling. Both he and Noella knew that for the sake of his children he had to return to his family and reconcile with his wife. He did. When Noella found out she was pregnant several weeks later, she never said a thing. She didn't want to ruin the man's first family. Yves and Yvette were born.

Now, twenty years later, the man's brother had come forward. It seemed both the man and his wife had passed on and he thought Yves and his sister would want to know the truth. It was a shock for the family, one they were still recovering from.

And now, Yves would have to tell his mother that he was a criminal.

"This isn't easy, Tania." Yves reached out and clasped her hand. "I've screwed up. It isn't easy on anyone. Do you think Kev's happy? Marc? Tyler? I mean, what are their families going to think?"

Despite all their money, their trips, their clothes, the four of them had managed to keep everything a secret, for the most part. Sylvie knew a little bit, but she was married to Kevin, how couldn't she? But everyone else, well . . . there may have been suspicions but nothing more. Everyone's family still thought they were top-notch guys.

No, this was not going to be easy on anyone.

Kevin? His mother was dead, so she wouldn't be hurt. Hell, figured Yves, that was one of the reasons Kevin went so far in this business. Marilyn Grandmaison had been big in her son's life, the two were tight. When she died, well, it kind of sucked the ambition right out of Kevin. He had already been doing a lot of small crimes, but when his mom died, it was like a floodgate opening and there was nothing holding him back. But if Kevin went down, his stepfather would not be too impressed. Ron Hart had married Kevin's mother when Kevin was just 10 years old, after his biological father had left, plagued by a lifetime of drinking problems. Hart, a building superintendent, had moved Marilyn, Kevin, his brother and sister around the Ottawa Valley from job to job. They landed in Cardinal for a couple of years, Iroquois for a few more and then headed to Ottawa. It had been a spotty upbringing, but Kevin and his step-dad had been pretty close. Yves was sure Kevin wouldn't be too thrilled about breaking that news to his old man.

Tyler? It was already hard on Tyler, harder maybe than it would be for Yves to break the news to Noella. Tyler had to call his mom from the St. Catharines jail to get the bail money. She wasn't pleased and had been riding her son hard ever since. It was no wonder, Yves thought. Tyler's mom was top class, a straight arrow who worked as a procurement officer with the federal government and provided him and his brother David with everything they needed as they grew up. With the father long out of the picture, it was just the three of them living in a townhouse off Pinecrest Avenue when they were growing up. Tyler's brother David had kept his nose clean, working as a manager at an Ottawa Travelodge, but now, just as his mother neared retirement, Tyler was in a whole heap of trouble. She knew about St. Catharines but remained in the dark about the Saanich bust, along with the extended version of the quartet's adventures in crime. If she attended his trial in St. Catharines, as she insisted she was going to do, that'd come up for sure. The Saanich bust was on record, and Tyler had little doubt it'd be used against him. His mother would kill Tyler, no question about it.

Marc? This was a huge mess for him, too. He hadn't told anyone yet either. His girlfriend, Terri Anne, knew of course, because she came down to St. Catharines. But his mom Darlene? She knew nothing. Yves couldn't tell quite how she would handle it. When they were growing up, when Yves used to hang out at Marc's place, Darlene was the coolest mom you could ask for. You could talk to her and if trouble came up, she was usually pretty understanding — "Boys will be boys," she'd laugh when he and Marc would come home from school cut or bruised, looking for some food after a scuffle. Darlene had practically raised Marc and his two brothers and sister by herself, bringing in money by running her own flower shop. They had grown up living in a nice townhouse on Poulin Avenue, in Ottawa's west end. Marc's dad, now he would probably be pissed. Nino Flamini had left the family when Marc was still a teenager, but they kept in touch. Nino had been a star athlete, even played club soccer with some big names in Italy. When he found out what his son had been up to . . . Yves didn't want to think about it. Poor Marc.

Yves drained the rest of his drink as the waitress came to clear the plates from the table. It was an ugly situation for all of them. The waitress waved menus in front of him and Tania, but neither were in the mood for dessert.

"I don't know what to say, Tania. Maybe it was the gambling, maybe it was the money, it just kept going," Yves continued to explain. His face was exhausted, robbed of any sign of lingering emotion. "Now I'm going to have to pay the price."

Tania looked up at him and smiled, then placed her hand on his muscled forearm. Her eyes lost in his, sincerity bubbling over, she choked out a couple tear-stained words, "We'll get through it Yves. Don't worry."

Y Y Y

Bowmaster leaned back in his wooden chair and looked at the digital clock that was sitting on the secretary's desk. The red face told a story he didn't want to hear. It was 2:45 a.m. Another night without seeing his wife and kids. Another night without a decent amount of sleep. He sighed and looked at the piles of photos and police reports that comprised the landscape of his desk. And there was so much more to do.

"Damn." He groaned and got up to start the coffee machine. No point even thinking about sleep.

It was the last weekend of March, six weeks after the St. Catharines bust. Fagan was on the road, trying to track down some witnesses in southern Ontario. They had both been working like dogs. Since Christmas Day, Bowmaster had had only one day off because of the investigation. Fagan was even worse. He took files home to read while his wife cooked the turkey for Christmas dinner. It was getting out of control.

Bowmaster tossed the clammy old coffee grinds into the garbage and fished out a satchel of Maxwell House.

While the coffee was brewing, he took a walk through the offices. They were working out of one of the houses the OPP owned in Ottawa. It was just another non-descript house on a non-descript block in Ottawa's west end, but it was quiet and most of the neighbours thought, if they thought anything, that it was an accountant's office. No marked police cars ever came here, only the plain-clothes guys in their sober Crown Victorias or Pontiac 6000s, guys like Bowmaster and Fagan.

The whole place had been set up just for Project Fiddler. There were maps on one wall with red pins marking all the suspected break-ins along with the possible driving routes to and from the various cities. Another wall was splashed with photos of Grandmaison, Belanger, Flamini and Wilson, taken by undercover agents. From each of the gang members' photos, lines were branching out to other photographs, those of suspected fences or others involved in the case some way.

Bowmaster rubbed the stubble growing on his chin. It'd been two or three days since he had had a chance to shave.

Slowly, but surely, they were building a strong case against these punks, with the St. Catharines job as the spool the threads were being wound on. In fact, the investigation was going better than Bowmaster and Fagan could have hoped.

Y Y Y

For the past two weeks, officers had been going back to each of the stores that they believed the gang had broken into, trying to get witnesses or evidence. They thought it would be a lost cause, with months, sometimes years, having passed since the gang broke into the stores. But they got lucky.

A typical case came in the second week of March when Fagan went to question staff at the Shoppers Drug Mart in Chatham, Ontario. The boys had hit the store for $45,000 on April 23, 1995. That had been 11 months ago so Fagan wasn't expecting much when he sat down with the employees.

He got little at first. The manager and assistant mangers remembered nothing and no matter how long they stared at the mug shots of Grandmaison, Belanger, Flamini and Wilson, they simply couldn't place those boys. It was the same story with the stock clerks and maintenance staff. But when Fagan got to the cashiers, it was a totally different story.

They were all young women, 16, 17, maybe 18, earning money for their first car or maybe to go to university or college. As soon as Fagan dropped the mug shots on the table, the girls reacted. The three of them who worked on April 22, 1995, the day before last year's robbery, pointed to the shots of Flamini and Wilson.

"I remember those guys. They were sooooo cute," murmured one cashier named Julie. She was a short, attractive girl with dyed-black hair in a short-cut bob, which hung nicely around her jawline, framing her face.

She remembered what they were wearing, what they said to her, what they bought — everything. After the guys had left the store, the cashiers had even gotten together and gossiped about them.

"You know, really good-looking guys don't come in here that often," Julie explained, smiling at the memory of the taller one. She wondered what his name was. Julie was excited, talking with the other girls. Maybe they'd get to go to court. A couple days off school.

"You ask," Julie said, nudging her friend.

"No you go, you go," Sarah, another cashier, whispered back, holding her giggles.

"Officer?" asked Julie.

"Yes," Fagan answered, while he was quickly scanning the layout of the store.

"Will we be, ah, will we get to be witnesses in court?"

Sarah giggled, while Julie stifled hers and tried to politely smile.

"There's a chance," Fagan answered. He was smiling too. This was a nice break from the paperwork, mug shots and never-ending details of a case that had exploded beyond anyone's expectations. "Nothing's sure yet, but you've helped me out a lot."

An early spring gust of warm air greeted him in the parking lot as he left the store. Breathing deeply, holding it in, warming his body and melting away the permafrost that seemed to have made his bones brittle, Fagan just savoured his good fortune. It happened again and again wherever Fagan went. The young girls in the store, whether they stocked shelves, swept the aisles or worked the cash, always remembered a group of dashing young men spending a couple of hours in the store a day or so before it got robbed. They had never made the connection before — they were too good-looking to be criminals, cooed one young blond admirer — but Fagan now had more than two dozen witnesses who could place Flamini and Wilson in stores at least 48 hours before they got hit.

The grunt work was starting to pay off too. They had another officer go get the car-rental records for every car the guys had rented, and then match the kilometres driven to what stores had been broken into that weekend. It certainly wouldn't be enough on its own, but in more than two dozen cases, the mileage on the rental car matched what it would take to do a round trip from Ottawa to the site of the job. It was circumstantial, but no judge would miss its significance.

They had another officer trying to get videotape of the guys. Before every job, they'd stop at a Canadian Tire and purchase the standard working equipment: an ordinary pickaxe, crowbars and screwdrivers. Bowmaster and Fagan had selected the 15 most recent jobs and sent the officer to the Canadian Tire closest to where the break-and-enter had occurred to see if they had kept the security camera videotape from around that date.

Six Canadian Tires had, and the officer watched the tapes. On two, he had been able to pick out the gang. On one, Belanger and Flamini were buying the tell-tale yellow dishwashing gloves and a pick at a Canadian Tire outside of St. Thomas, Ontario. In the other videotape, it was Flamini and Wilson buying screwdrivers, duct tape and crowbars at a Canadian Tire in Sudbury one day before a Shoppers got hit there. The tapes were grainy and black and white, but there was no mistaking those faces. The tapes, combined with the one they had already recovered of the three guys dressed in black sliding across one drug store floor to avoid the motion detectors, would make for good, solid courtroom viewing.

Y Y Y

The whirring of the coffee machine stopped, leaving the office silent. Bowmaster headed back to pour himself a tall mug. He was wearing a white Project Fiddler T-shirt and a pair of faded blue jeans. Whenever the OPP got involved in a major project, someone — usually the communications staff who worked transcribing the phone taps — printed up a bunch of shirts and sold them to the officers involved in the case. When Bowmaster looked through his closet, all he needed to do was check out his T-shirts and it was like reading his resumé. The Fiddler shirts had a picture of a fiddle on the front, then on the back, a list of the things the guys would repeatedly say during their phone conversations, things that the communications staff got sick and tired of hearing. There was "Smell you later," and "Knock, buddy," a reference to the gang's relentless superstition about knocking on wood whenever discussing any criminal activity, and a host of other inane phrases that the guys used.

Bowmaster returned to his desk and started thumbing through the stack of hotel indexes. These were another good source of evidence. Although the gang had been smart enough to use fake names once in a while, there were still a lot of rooms they could connect to the gang. In fact, they already had 16 rooms registered to Grandmaison, nine to Wilson, six to Flamini and four to Belanger. Bowmaster was pretty sure these rooms represented only the tip of the iceberg, and it was pretty easy to guess where else they had been. All he had to do was call the major hotels in the city which had been hit, and see if they had any reports of room damage or guests who skipped out on phone bills around the time of the break-in. Voila.

The guys must have thought they were rock stars. They trashed their hotel rooms, sometimes leaving huge holes gouged out of the walls and the beds broken. And even though they had "earned" tens of thousands of dollars for their night's work, they always skipped out on their phone bills. Every single time.

Bowmaster picked up copies of the phone records from rooms

that hadn't settled their bills and sure enough, there were calls made to Ottawa addresses that could be connected to the gang, whether it was their girlfriends, their friends or their business partners.

Again, it was circumstantial, but once Bowmaster and Fagan showed the judge the mountain of circumstance connecting the gang to the crimes, it would be as solid as a smoking gun and an eyewitness.

The phone taps and bugs in Grandmaison's apartment were also beginning to reap their rewards. There were thousands of hours of tape — those four guys seemed to live on the phone — but even though they were trying to be careful, the gang had given up some good information.

In one of the most frustrating chapters of the entire case, Bowmaster and Fagan thought they could sink the gang with one hour of tape.

All four had met in Kevin's apartment to discuss their predicament. They knew they were in trouble, what with having gone down in St. Catharines, and they wanted to make sure they had their stories straight to tell their lawyers.

Bowmaster and Fagan heard the start of the conversation through the bugs, right up until when Kevin said "Here's what we're going to tell our lawyers . . . ."

That's when Sylvie, who was home in the other room, turned on the stereo and stuck in a CD. Whoever had planted the bug in the room had left it too close to one of the speakers. While the guys talked about hell knows what, the technicians were left listening to bad pop music played far too loud. Another technician later identified the music as the Alanis Morissette CD, but that meant nothing to Bowmaster and Fagan. What meant something was that the tape was totally unusable. By the time the CD finished playing the guys were talking about the upcoming hockey playoffs and their plans for partying that night.

It was like a sick joke.

But in a different, happy twist, the case had become a whole lot clearer a couple of weeks back. Bowmaster and Fagan had been a bit confused by a rash of jobs in Toronto — about a dozen rooftop jobs were reported to them that didn't have quite the same modus operandi. Instead of breaking through the roof, the perpetrators went through the air conditioning ducts and snuck into the store. It was a tight squeeze but the stores were usually hit for about $25,000.

Bowmaster and Fagan were pretty sure these jobs weren't their guys. It didn't make sense that they'd switch their routine for just the Toronto jobs. But still, they had sent officers to check out the files.

It turned out to be a completely different gang, and the Metro cops took them down in February. It never ceased to amaze Bowmaster how many punks there were in the world.

He drained the rest of his coffee, but it was a useless gesture. The long hours and litres of coffee had long since numbed his body to the wondrous effects of caffeine. All he really wanted to do was lie down.

He checked the digital clock again. 4:23 a.m.

Bowmaster got up and went to the long, orange sofa in the corner of the office and laid down.

"Fuck it," he spoke to himself out loud as he rested his head against the couch's arm. "The investigation is on chart. I deserve a couple of hours' shut-eye."

Y Y Y

"You guys can get some rest now. We're home. By the way, that guy in the blue car today? He was a bit too fucking obvious. Let's get some professionals on the job, OK?"

Kevin slammed down the phone. Those fucking pricks. Like he didn't know they were being taped and followed. He went over to the window of the apartment he and Sylvie shared and twisted open the blinds. There were a couple of cars on the street and damn, if that station wagon didn't look familiar. If the guys had been suspicious before the St. Catharines job, they were certain they were being tailed now.

The cops in St. Catharines hadn't mentioned any jobs other than the Shoppers, but it wouldn't take a genius to figure out that there had been a couple of other jobs done in the area the exact same way. If the police were real smart, they could even check out some of the other unsolved crime reports from across the province, put two and two together and deduce that they had some real hot suspects on their hands. Even these fucking jokers could get that far.

Still, Kevin was confident the pricks couldn't connect the four of them to the other crimes. They were clean jobs, no prints, no witnesses. And the guys were solid, nobody would say a thing. Of course, he knew the cops would try. And that meant the phone taps and the tail.

So far, they had been obvious. It was pretty much the same group of cops following them. What did they think they'd find? Did they think he was so stupid that he'd go out and do a job right before their eyes? The bastards.

Not that he wasn't tempted. He was nearly tapped out. He had cashed in most of his bonds and GICs to pay down the bookies. They were off his back. For now. Kevin also blew some of his dwindling reserves to go down to Acapulco the first week of April with Tyler, Yves and some other friends. A little stress reliever, one which Kevin could justify. Other than that, he and Sylvie were living off their credit cards.

Tyler and Marc were all right. They had some money stashed away. Yves, well, he was real anxious to work again. But for now, with the heat on so bad, there was nothing they could do.

What was worse was the idea of paying lawyers. They would have to hook up with someone real soon. Marc had gotten a friend's lawyer for the bail hearing in St. Catharines, but they would need someone else for the trial. They already had their stories straight, so it'd just be a matter of money.

Kevin stayed at the window, glaring down at the parked cars.

Everyone was laying low right now, real low. Marc had actually moved in with Terri Anne, Yves practically lived at Tania's, and Tyler and Kerri were getting pretty serious again.

"Kevin, come on back to bed. Stop worrying about them outside."

Kevin turned to Sylvie. "You're right. Fuck it. They can't touch us."

Y Y Y

Sitting in his tiny office in the depths of the Ottawa police station on Elgin Street, Staff Sgt. Lance Valcour could barely keep from smiling.

Just six months ago, he had been chosen to lead the force's break-and-enter squad. After years of skyrocketing break-and-enter statistics and more and more complaints from the community, Ottawa-Carleton police decided to change the way they dealt with the crimes.

Domestic break-and-enters were by far the most common crime in the city and by far the crime that people got angriest about. It was upsetting to read about a murder in the newspaper, but absolutely traumatizing to come home after a night of euchre at a friend's house to find your window smashed and your VCR, TV and CDs gone.

But for the most part, there was little the police could do about them. They were usually executed by crackheads or teenagers looking for some quick spending money. They operated loosely and late at night, and even if kids were caught, they faced only a slap on their wrists for their first couple of offenses.

Commercial break-and-enters weren't much better. Their numbers were also on the rise and the criminals who executed those were usually professional, with a system of fences and network of contacts. The force had limited success in taking some of these groups down, but clearly, the system wasn't working.

So the Ottawa-Carleton police initiated a brand new police enterprise, the Break and Enter Response Team, or BERT as it was called around the station. Based on the theory that four per cent of the criminals were responsible for eighty per cent of the break-ins, Valcour shaped BERT so it could attack the most serious offenders and eliminate the majority of the crimes.

The plan was relatively simple: Go after the known criminals and devote their time to the break-and-enters that had the best chance of being solved. Valcour even had a system where he would rank every break-in conducted in the his region — the cities of Ottawa, Nepean, Gloucester and Vanier — on a "solvability scale." It was quite a task, considering that in 1995 there were more than 11,000 break-ins in the region.

Valcour, a boyish-looking detective in his late 30s, was one of the most industrious and hard-working cops on the force. After six months of eighty-hour weeks and butting heads to get his new system in place, it was beginning to work. Since BERT had been formed in October, break-ins in the Ottawa-Carleton area were down by an incredible 48 per cent. That kind of statistic made Valcour ecstatic.

What shot him into absolute euphoria was the help he was going to get from Project Fiddler.

There was nothing more expensive for police to do than "string a wire" — put down bugs and wire taps in suspects' apartments. Valcour would have needed a sensational case to get the force to grant him the budget to get that kind of surveillance. But with OPP and their million-dollar budget for Project Fiddler, they had wires down and the break-and-enter team had access to everything. Every day when he read the transcripts of the taped phone conversations, he learned a little something new, a little something that would help the team put somebody away, if not now, later. He could already identify at least 10 arrests the squad could make once the case broke wide open.

It wasn't that much of a surprise to him to see Grandmaison, Belanger, Flamini and Wilson at the centre of the investigation. They were, in cop jargon, "known to police." To get them off the Ottawa streets would be especially sweet for Valcour.

Yes, this was turning out to be a good year. First the success of his break-and-enter team, now the Project Fiddler wire taps falling right into his lap. Maybe, just maybe, they were starting to turn the tide in the war against crime.

Y Y Y

Sylvie lay asleep, her head on Kevin's shoulder and her long brown hair cascading across his chest. The sun had risen, just, but with their bedroom windows facing the west, the room remained dark and quiet.

The pounding at first seemed part of a dream. Sylvie and Kevin had planned to go down to Jamaica for a week together —they knew they shouldn't, considering their finances — and Sylvie dreamt of the trip, her mother, a tropical beach and the sound of a canoe slapping against a sun-weathered dock. Then, as the dream shifted and swirled into a mess of colours and memories, the pounding got louder. This was no dream.

"Kevin. Wake up." She was a little scared. "What's that noise?" She shifted in her bed and propped herself up on one arm, the sheets tumbling from her body, leaving her breasts exposed. She listened again. The pounding came again, this time louder.

It was the door.

The clock read 6:39 a.m., an ungodly hour. She shook Kevin awake. "Kevin. There's someone at the door."

Kevin nodded sleepily, and got up, slipping on a pair of zebra-patterned boxer shorts from Joe Boxer. He felt his way to the door, which was trembling beneath the pounding. Through the peephole stood a grizzled man with a beard, a biker-type that Kevin had never seen before.

Startled awake, Kevin rushed back to the bedroom, suddenly alert, as adrenaline began pumping through his body.

"Sylv, come on, out of bed," he whispered urgently. "Answer the door, and whatever you do, don't tell anyone I'm here."

Sylvie looked shaken but pulled on a terrycloth robe and went to the door. Making sure the chain was firmly in place, she opened it a crack. "Who is it?"

"It's the goddamn police. Get the door open. Now."

Sylvie panicked and slammed the door shut.

She ran to the bedroom.

"Kevin . . ." she started, but before any more words would come out, a crashing slap of thunder shot in from the main room as the front door was smashed in. The biker-type walked in first, displaying a badge in one hand and his Glock pistol in the other.

Sylvie did a double-take. It was the man who had stood behind her in line yesterday at the drycleaners. The same man who was at the Loeb last week. And who was sitting in the Dodge Ram outside their house one morning. He had been following them.

Before Sylvie could react, the biker was joined by four uniformed officers, each with his gun drawn.

"Kevin Grandmaison, you are under arrest for break-and-enter with intent, conspiracy to commit break-and-enter, conspiracy to commit robbery . . . ."

The charges kept coming and coming. Kevin couldn't believe his ears. "What the hell is this? What the hell is going on?"

The biker smiled a wide grin. "Your games are over, Kevin. Put on some clothes. You're coming with us."

Sixty seconds later, after throwing on some jeans and a Polo pullover, Kevin was gone. Sylvie, alone and in her terrycloth robe, picked up a broom and dustpan to begin cleaning up the splinters from the broken door. A steady stream of tears soaked her face.

It was still early on the same morning of April 24th when police arrived at Marc's apartment and yanked him from the warm futon he was sharing with Terri Anne. Tyler was next, awakened by the incessant buzzer of his apartment door, and then searched and cuffed while his girlfriend Kerri looked on helplessly. Yves was the last one picked up, and the only one who had the dignity of being fully clothed when arrested. Just after 7 a.m., Yves had left Tania's place and was driving back to his apartment when the police pulled him over. He was prepared for a simple license check — he had about 20 outstanding parking tickets — instead, he was cuffed and forced into the back seat of the cruiser.

The four were hustled out to the OPP station in Kanata and put through the paces. Bowmaster and Fagan sat and watched the whole process, quick to inform them of how much they had on them.

"We've got 40 good cases against you guys. You're ours now."

By the end of the day, the Ottawa-Carleton police made 15 more arrests, all as a result of information from the wiretaps. Friends of the gang were arrested, men who fenced the stolen stamps were arrested, even some girls were arrested.

Jennifer Hayes, Marc's one-time girlfriend, was charged with conspiracy because she had rented a car for the gang. Sylvie was arrested in her apartment 12 hours after Kevin had been taken away, having been nailed with charges of conspiracy to commit robbery, conspiracy to commit break-and-enter and conspiracy to commit theft over $5,000.

It was information the police were not shy about sharing with the boys as they were being prepared to be shipped to jail.

"All your little friends will be joining you, don't worry," chuckled Fagan as he watched Grandmaison, Belanger, Flamini and Wilson being loaded into the transport van.

With hard metal handcuffs stinging their wrists and shackles weighing down their ankles, the van carrying the four of them to jail was unnaturally quiet. Even Yves kept his mouth shut, his eyes cast on the van's floor.

Finally, it was Marc, who had shown so much bravado weeks before in St. Catharines, who broke the stillness. Leaning forward, he did little more than whisper: "They seem to be taking this quite seriously."

Chapter NINE

July 1996
Ottawa, Ontario

Fagan jammed on the accelerator and peeled out of the underground parking lot of the Ottawa courthouse, leaving two fresh stripes of smoking rubber smouldering on the concrete floor.

"Ratfuckers."

As he swerved onto Laurier Avenue and headed west, he pounded his fist against the wheel of the white Crown Victoria and looked over at Bowmaster. His partner wore an angry scowl and was yanking a navy-blue tie from his neck.

"That little prick Marin. I can't believe he wants to cut a goddamn deal."

Bowmaster rubbed his temple and nodded. This was no good. No good at all. They hadn't gotten a single break since the major set of charges had been laid.

First off, because the gang's crimes had been committed in so many different jurisdictions, there was some uncertainty as to where the trial would be held. Bowmaster and Fagan had wanted to get the gang tried in Barrie, or Hazard Country as it is affectionately known among Ontario's criminals. The Crown's office up there was legendary for its harsh sentences and zero tolerance for little prick criminals. Bowmaster and Fagan were positive Grandmaison, Belanger, Flamini and Wilson would be looking at 10 years in a federal penitentiary if their case was tried there. The Crown's office in Barrie had balls.

When they got the news that the trial was going to be held in Ottawa, because it was the guys' hometown and there had been several break-ins committed in the region, it was a blow. The Crown's office in Ottawa had too many soft liberals in it who let too many hard criminals get away with light sentences.

Still, it wasn't the end of the world. Even if the trial was held in Ottawa, Fagan and Bowmaster were sure the gang would get at least five years, once all the evidence was given in court, the victim impact statements read, and the gang's massive network of criminal contacts revealed. Once the investigation was finally completed, the four men faced charges in connection with a little more than 50 break-and-enters. And then everyone around them, a whole entourage of their friends, were facing charges ranging from conspiracy to commit break-and-enter to possession of stolen property to fraud and uttering forged documents.

It seemed a safe bet that they'd get hard time. A five-year sentence would mean the boys would be going to a federal institution, a concept that Bowmaster and Fagan loved to think about. Once those pretty boys walked into a federal penitentiary, it would be the education of their lives. There was no doubt the handsome types, especially Flamini, would quickly become some con's woman on the inside. That would shut his mouth. For once.

But now, after a two-hour meeting with the Crown's office and Andre Marin, the attorney handling the case, their worst nightmare had come true. The Crown wanted a deal; there would be no trial.

The car was silent as Fagan continued down Laurier, headed for The Prescott, one of Ottawa's oldest taverns. You could always count on relaxing with a cold glass of Canadian at The Prescott, and after today's meeting they both felt like several.

Fagan turned onto Preston Street and parked the car on a side road near the tavern. When they opened the doors, the blessedly cool, air-conditioned air of the Crown Victoria spun away into the late July sun and Bowmaster and Fagan were hit with a blast of muggy heat. It was a hot summer in Ottawa, and as usual, the humidity was a killer. By the time they had walked the half-block to The Prescott, both men were dripping sweat and grateful for the cool, dark air of the tavern. They slipped through the doors, checked the room for any friends, then sat at one of the long, brown Formica tables near the door. Mitch the bartender waved at them and brought over a pitcher of Canadian and two glasses.

Fagan took a long pull on his beer and turned to his partner. "I just don't understand this, Bow. I know the money's tight, but shit. We got a good case on those little fuckers. It should go to trial."

Bowmaster nodded. They had a *great* case on those little fuckers.

Aside from the more than 30 witnesses Bowmaster and Fagan had identified who could place the gang in the same city as the crimes, they had the videotape, the wiretap information and file cases full of circumstantial evidence, right down to the odometer readings on the cars the gang rented.

But all that evidence meant a lot of work getting the information before a judge. It would mean the Crown would have to fly all the witnesses into Ottawa for the trial, present all the evidence and open it up to examination. It would likely mean a year in court. That would mean millions of dollars just to prosecute the pricks.

Marin certainly wasn't happy with the prospect of that much time and that much money. With blond hair and youthful good looks, Marin was easily the most ambitious attorney in the Ottawa office. He thrived on the high-profile trials that would get his name in the newspapers and his face on TV and was constantly looking for ways to move up the ladder. Getting saddled with a year-long break-and-enter trial was a thought that didn't please him. And the money that would be spent didn't please the Crown's comptroller. Marin was given his marching orders: Go get a deal.

As he sat with Bowmaster and Fagan in his cramped office on the third floor of the Ottawa courthouse, he laid down the plan.

The Crown was still going to ask for federal time. Four years minimum. The bottom line was that the trial was too expensive and that these kids were first-time offenders with no record of violence. It was all property offenses, covered by insurance.

Marin raised his hands, his gesture of resignation. More like defeat, Bowmaster thought.

"Look, guys, it's not the Texas chainsaw massacre we're dealing with here. Considering the dead time, it means they're going to serve a pretty severe sentence. I think they'll learn crime loses its glamour when you're inside a jail."

What could Bowmaster and Fagan do? They knew that Marin's hopes of getting a four-year sentence for the gang was a crock of shit.

If that was what the Crown would demand, then the result would be somewhere in between that and what the defence wanted. The guys had some smart lawyers on their side and there was no way they would accept the Crown's initial offer. When the dust settled after negotiations, the guys could plead to as little as two-and-a-half or three years.

Bowmaster refilled their glasses while Fagan got up to use The Prescott's bathrooms.

It had been 13 weeks since the gang had been arrested for the second time, roused from their beds just after the break of dawn. A search of their apartments after the arrests had yielded more evidence, but not as much as Bowmaster and Fagan had hoped.

In Grandmaison and Flamini's apartments, they had found some commemorative hockey coins that had been reported stolen from a break-and-enter at a Shoppers Drug Mart in Pickering in 1995. That made Bowmaster chuckle. The four of them had always been sports nuts so it didn't surprise him that they had kept the coins.

In Wilson's apartment, they had found stamps and lottery tickets. The stamps were positively identified as coming from the Groombridge Sampler Outlet in Sarnia, whose roof had been cut and safe had been cracked in June 1995. The lottery tickets were traced back to two different sources: a Shoppers Drug Mart in Strathroy that had been broken into in October 1995 and a Shoppers Drug Mart in Sudbury that had been broken into in January 1996.

Belanger had no solid evidence in his apartment, but the officers did find a police scanner and a book of police frequencies for the province of Ontario. That was damning in itself.

The new evidence, plus the St. Catharines job, plus the evidence gathered by Project Fiddler, plus the hundreds of breaches of the non-association clause in their bail contract was enough for any judge. After the April arrests, Grandmaison, Belanger, Flamini and Wilson had been denied bail and were left roasting in the Barrie jail all summer.

It now looked like the trial was scheduled for the first week of September, but if Marin got his deal, it would be the mere formality of the four boys appearing in court to officially receive their sentence. It was one of the many frustrations of police work for Bowmaster. They spent all their time tracking the criminals, preparing the evidence, getting the little shits off the streets. Then, when it came time to be punished, the little fucks got no more than a slap on the wrist. It was a slap in the face to police, that's what it was. It was a slap in the face of justice. How would these fucks ever learn to respect the law when it treated hard-core criminals like they were children in kindergarten?

Fagan reappeared, another pitcher of Canadian in his hand even though the first one still wasn't done.

What the hell, figured Bowmaster. This was definitely a two-or three-pitcher day. It just meant they wouldn't be driving home.

Y Y Y

As August turned to September, the gang's trial finally was in sight. It was a great relief for all of them.

After their arrests on the morning of April 24th, they had been kept at the Ottawa-Carleton Regional Detention Centre on Innes Road for a day and then packed into vans for the long ride out to the Barrie Jail or the Barrie bucket as it was not-so-affectionately known. The place was a hell-hole, one of the oldest jails in the province, with idiot thugs in almost every cell and guards with an attitude. Even worse, it was more than 400 kilometres and a five-hour drive from home, too far for their girlfriends, their friends or even their families to make regular visits.

They'd spent five horrible weeks in Barrie before being transferred back to Ottawa in June so they could consult more freely with their lawyers and be prepared for the start of the trial. The rest of summer, June, July and August, was spent at Innes Road, while the trial date was being set and then postponed, and then set again. It was weeks of useless, monotonous jail time, with their lawyers buzzing about like fruit flies around a rotting bunch of bananas.

The most frustrating part for the four of them was that it was all dead time. With no trial and no conviction, they were being held in jail simply because a judge had considered their crimes too severe and their disregard for the law too great to release them before their trial. It had been four-and-a-half useless months, just wasted time spent behind bars.

The trial date that had finally been decided on was September 13th. It was a Friday. A horrible omen. When that came down, in the last sweaty week of August, the four of them had huddled on the basketball court at the detention centre to come up with a plan. What kind of luck would they have on Friday the 13th? None of them wanted to find out. But when Yves and Kevin told their lawyers they were considering asking for a change of date, their lawyers warned them it could take another six weeks for a court date to open up that the three lawyers, the Crown Attorney and the judge could attend. They were stuck with Friday the 13th.

With the date set, all that was left was for their lawyers to meet with Marin and see if they could work out a deal.

The four of them had hired some of the biggest law firms in eastern Ontario to represent them, an act that ate away the majority of any cash they had stashed away.

Richard Addelman was representing Kevin and Tyler. He was huge, one of the top criminal lawyers in the region. Addelman had handled a long list of high-profile drinking and driving cases which saw his clients receive light or no sentences. He also wrangled an absurdly light sentence — nine months — for a 15-year-old boy who went on a shooting rampage in the village of Dunrobin, Ontario. One of the cases that drew Kevin and Tyler to Addelman was when, in the early 1990s, he had sprung a man from a shoddy murder charge. Police had said his client, Luc Pilon, had bludgeoned and stabbed to death a man in a wheelchair using, among other things, an ice pick. Addelman had it thrown out of court before the cops knew what hit them.

It was costing Kevin and Tyler a lot of money, but they believed they had made a sound investment.

Yves had gone right to the top, hiring the firm of Michael Edelson & Associates. Edelson and his team of lawyers had consistently done the impossible for clients. They had gotten not guilty verdicts for Serge Loranger, an OPP officer who had allegedly pounded back a dozen pints of beer at a bar, drove home, running down and killing a teenager on a bicycle on the way. They had also successfully defended RCMP Sgt. Earl Blair Taker, who was connected to another alcohol-related accident which left two women with critical injuries.

In the most sensational criminal case in Ottawa's history, the random drive-by shooting of Nicholas Battersby on Elgin Street, Edelson had represented the driver of the Jeep and negotiated a light sentence. Edelson's name was burned in the mind of every criminal in eastern Ontario as a lawyer who could get the job done, and Belanger didn't want to mess around. For Belanger's break-and-enter charges, Edelson had put one of his top guns on the case, Connie D'Angelo.

Marc had hooked up with a lawyer who wasn't quite in the same league as Addelman and Edelson. Mark Ertel was a young criminal lawyer, a hot shot who had handled cases for some of Marc's friends who owned bars in the Market area of Ottawa. He had handled a couple of big cases — he got an arson case thrown out of court after obliterating the police evidence in court, and handled a client involved in the bitter internal dispute at Interval House, an Ottawa home for battered women — but his star was still rising. On the word of his friends, Marc trusted Ertel with his life.

As Labour Day came and went and the September days continued to pass, there was less confusion about the gang's future. By now, Marin had made it clear, he wanted a deal. All that was left for Addelman, D'Angelo and Ertel was to negotiate the conditions and how long the sentence would be. The gang had the edge in these discussions: they knew how badly the Crown wanted a deal and if they didn't get what they wanted, they would force the trial.

The Crown would spend millions.

The gang would get killed in legal fees, and everything they ever said or did would be on public display — in court and in the local newspapers.

Nobody wanted to see it go that far.

Y Y Y

Marc stood and looked out the cell door. They had been waiting forever, having been shipped over from Innes Road at 8:30 in the morning. They were stripped down and searched before getting on the van, taken in through the basement door of the courthouse and shoved in a holding cell. Now it was some time after 11 a.m. and they were still sitting in the bland white cell with a bunch of other rejects who were awaiting trial. They were supposed to appear at 10 a.m. What was happening?

CHAPTER NINE

Everyone thought there would be a deal in place by now. Almost everything had been sorted out. The four of them would agree to plead guilty to 54 cases of break-and-enter and also, although they would not go down as crimes attributed to any of them, the police would close the cases on more than a hundred other break-and-enters in Ontario and British Columbia. That meant that nobody, especially any of them, could be charged with those crimes. As well, a deal was reached that the four accused could not be charged with any other break-and-enter crime committed prior to the date of their arrest in the provinces of British Columbia and Ontario that might surface later on.

That was the good part of the deal, and it made Marc smile. There was some concern about the jobs that had been committed outside those two provinces. At one point, while the four of them were under interrogation by Bowmaster and Fagan, Kevin and Yves had even tried to raise the issue of these other crimes, but with no result. Bowmaster and Fagan had simply told them to keep quiet — they had deals in British Columbia and Ontario, but the police couldn't promise them anything else.

With the police work out of the way, all that was left was the punishment. The Crown wanted four years. Addelman seemed to think the best they could do was get two years. But Yves's lawyer, D'Angelo, was convinced that they could get two years less a day, a sentence that would allow them to serve their time in the more relaxed atmosphere of a provincial jail. They had arrived at court expecting the length of the sentence to be resolved. But still nothing.

They waited another half-hour, too nervous to talk, just sitting and watching the guards, lawyers and shackled prisoners pass outside the cell.

Marc continued to hang near the cell door, while Yves tried to nap on one of the benches. Kevin and Tyler sat in the opposite corner, keeping an eye on the other men in the cell.

Then, finally, Addelman appeared. The four of them gathered at the bars to hear what the lawyer had to say.

"They're adamant. Four years. I know it sounds bad, but remember: parole is a hell of a lot sweeter in the federal system than the provincial system."

Marc just laughed. That was a garbage offer.

Kevin spoke first. "No way. A deuce less a day or no deal."

Addelman shrugged and left. It was what he expected them to say and had told the Crown that. But he had to take them the offer just for show.

Tyler and Yves went back to the benches while Kevin stayed with Marc at the cell door.

"We'll get better than that. There's no way we won't."

Marc nodded before responding. "He's right about parole though."

It was true. In the provincial system, an inmate was eligible for parole after one-third of their sentence. In the federal system, inmates were eligible for day parole after one-sixth of their sentence. Then there was the issue of dead time. If they got a federal sentence, the time they had spent in jail could potentially be traded off and count towards their release date. No chance of that in the provincial system.

"Yeah, we'd get the parole quicker, but do you really want to do a pen bit?"

Marc only laughed. Who would?

Another hour passed. It was Addelman again who came down. Now the offer was two years. "They're really insistent on federal time. They'll give you two years. That's a real sweet deal. You should jump on it."

It was decision time. Two years wasn't a bad deal. But through it all, D'Angelo had insisted they should be offered two years less a day, considering their non-violent crimes, their lack of criminal records and the amount of money that was at stake if the trial was to go ahead. After a few minutes discussing it, just to make sure everyone was on the same page, they agreed. What was the point in saying yes now? If two years was on the table at noon, it would be on the table at the end of the day as well. They had nothing to lose. Tyler and Kevin went back to speak to their lawyer.

"No. No deal," said Tyler.

"We can do better," finished Kevin.

Addelman only shook his head and walked away. "It's a good deal," he said over his shoulder. "I don't think you'll get any better."

Another two hours passed. The guys drank watery coffee out of Styrofoam cups and ate processed ham on slices of Wonderbread. The food at the holding cells was even worse than at the jail.

At 3 p.m., Addelman made a final appearance. He raised his hands and shrugged. "You guys can be pricks, you know that?" Addelman said smiling at his clients. "It's on the table. Two years less a day."

Kevin smiled right back for just a second, and then the four of them spoke almost as one. "Yes." They had what they wanted. As they were being led up to the prisoner's box, Addelman had one last warning for them.

"Look, the Crown wants this and we want this. It's 99 per cent done. It should go . . . but remember. It's Belanger."

Justice Paul Belanger. One of the toughest on the Ottawa circuit. Not only that, but in pre-trial motions, he had been furious with the scope of the men's crimes.

He would not sleep, he promised the lawyers present, if the those punks got less than four years in a federal penitentiary. The Crown and defence had a deal, but it still awaited the approval of a judge who didn't seem to want to give it.

As they headed into the courtroom, each took long looks at the visitors' benches. Tyler's mom was there, so was Marc's. That was no surprise. They had been behind their sons each step, even kicking in some money for lawyers' fees. Yves looked for Noella, but she wasn't there. He shrugged it off. She had been devastated by the news, especially when it went into the papers. Coming to the trial would be too much stress for her. Their girlfriends were there of course — Sylvie, Tania, Terri Anne and Kerri. There were also about a half-dozen of their friends, some of whom faced their own charges because of Project Fiddler. The four of them sat down in the prisoners box and waited for the judge. This was it.

Y Y Y

Judge Belanger took his seat behind the bench. After nodding to the lawyers involved, he turned to the four accused and ordered them to rise. After hearing a simple statement from Glen Bowmaster and the details of the deal worked out between the Crown and the defence, Judge Belanger was ready to deliver his sentence. Kevin took a deep breath. He looked at Marc, who was fidgeting with his fingers and then Yves who was biting his lip. Tyler had his eyes closed. Everyone was nervous. Judge Belanger began speaking:

> Well gentlemen, all good things come to an end and today it seems is the end for you.
>
> One of your lawyers mentioned that you are not typical and perhaps that permitted you to do more than normally might be the case. Indeed, you are not typical. You are intelligent young men, you have apparent good families. You were born, I am sure, with a bit of a silver spoon, if not an entire one, in your mouths.
>
> I deal on a regular basis with young people who have never had a chance in life because of being abused, or because of having no family or because of any number of factors: being stupid or being born with disabilities. None of that can be said for you and, therefore, your situation is much more serious than would normally be the case with a 16-year-old. You are no spring chickens, any one of you; you are all between 23 and 28 years old.
>
> We have heard about business losses. Indeed, the staff sergeant tells us that some businesses went broke or were not able to start again because of you; they are the losers in that sense. But the biggest losers are not the businesses and the victims of these offenses, the four losers are here standing before me because the four of you have thrown away your lives.
>
> You have been traitors to your families who are here still supporting you, and to your girlfriends and wife. And you have let them down, and you have let them down in a big way.

Kevin felt dizzy. His stomach was clenched. He wanted to look at Sylvie, but he knew he couldn't turn around. The judge made it seem so bad. His face was flushed and he felt his eyes begin to water. That bastard. He could see Marc out of the corner of his eye. He was nervously patting his hair. Judge Belanger kept reading.

> But more important than that, you have let the four of yourselves down.
>
> Try and get a job in the future. Your lawyers talk with some degree of optimism about future employment. Well I can tell you, if I was an employer and I knew that any of you had spent two years in jail, I would not be anxious to have you working for me.
>
> The thing is that none of you have an excuse; you have all done it to yourselves. I cannot say as I did to another young man who appeared before you while you were in the back there that, well, he made a big mistake but everybody makes mistakes. In your case, 54, whatever it is, number of break-and-enters with $1.5 million as the total loss, those are not mistakes. A mistake happens once or twice, but not 54 times.

> The enormity of your crimes cries out, in fact, for a much lengthier term than has been proposed to me. And I would not be on dangerous ground, I think, with any court of appeal, even for first offenders in your age range, to consider penitentiary terms in the order of four and five years.

Whoa. Kevin was floored. He thought they had a deal. He looked to his lawyer, but Addelman wouldn't make eye contact. The judge sounded goddamn serious. He shut his eyes. If he had to do pen time, he would freak. He needed to go to the bathroom.

> I must, however, consider that this comes to me as a joint submission which has the support of the Crown Attorney's office, and perhaps the begrudging support of the police officers who are faced with the reality of prosecuting these cases, the reality of paying for them and knowing that these matters would take up many hundreds of hours of court time across this province. Most likely because of realism and experience, they reluctantly come to the conclusion that they ought to support what is being proposed to me today, and do so perhaps holding

their noses and wishing that this was a perfect world where we had the resources to prosecute each and every one of you to the full extent of the law.

Despite that, I am directed by our Court of Appeal to consider early pleas and to consider co-operation, and I must say that there has been co-operation in this case. I have to consider the fact that none of you have criminal records, and that while these offenses were extremely serious, they did not involve bodily harm to others or gratuitous damage.

The fact remains, gentleman, that your foolishness and your greed and whatever motivation has resulted in very very significant property losses; already, I am sure, many hundreds of hours in investigating these offenses and therefore, many many thousands of dollars to the public purse investigating these cases and eventually solving them.

As I say, when the proposition was first put to me in pre-trial, I felt that this clearly deserved penitentiary time. I have to bear in mind the fact that you have spent six months in pre-trial custody which, had you been serving post-sentence, would mean that you would have been entitled to be released after one-third of that one year. Therefore, in total calculation, that is a factor that I must bear in mind.

I accept this joint submission made to me with reluctance but, nevertheless, I am not saying it is improper. It is at the low end of the scale but it recognizes a number of factors I have mentioned.

Kevin stared right at the judge. This was it. The next years of his life were going to be told to him right there. Like a kid who wants to know what the future holds, it was there.

Mr. Flamini, you are sentenced to a term in jail of two years less one day, and three years probation.

Mr. Grandmaison, you are sentenced to a term in jail

> of two years less one day followed by three years probation.
>
> Similarly for you, Mr. Belanger, two years less one day in jail, followed by three years probation.
>
> And similarly for you, Mr. Wilson, two years in jail less one day, three years probation.

Kevin bowed his head and maintained a sombre facade. But his heart was leaping. They had got it. The son of a bitch judge had scared the shit out of him, but they had got what they wanted. Hot damn.

He turned to meet eyes with the others. They all had straight faces but Kevin could tell they were ecstatic. Yves was looking all over the courtroom, eyes on fire. Marc had a stone face but his foot was tapping a joyful beat. And Tyler, he was even beginning to crack a bit of a smile.

Yes.

Kevin caught Sylvie's eye. He winked.

This was not so bad after all.

Chapter TEN

Set deep amongst the green fields of the Ottawa Valley, a kilometre or so north of the winding Rideau River, sits the Rideau Correctional and Treatment Centre. Only a 45-minute drive from downtown Ottawa, the facility is nestled between farmers' fields and the picturesque town of Burritts Rapids.

As one of Ontario's medium-security jails, it is home to roughly 300 men who society has determined dangerous enough to put behind bars but not so menacing as to lock away in a federal penitentiary. Men who serve their time here have been convicted of offenses ranging from theft, break-and-enter or assault to dangerous driving causing death or even the occasional case of manslaughter.

It is considered by those familiar with such things as one of the easiest rides in the entire correctional system. There are no harsh, steel cells here. Inmates are kept in dormitories, long rooms with white walls and white bars on the windows that have enough beds for 26 men, along with a table where they can play cards, sit and chat or simply watch the hockey playoffs on television. There is lots of free time for inmates to play basketball, floor hockey or work out in the weight room that is all part of the complex's athletic centre. For those inclined to less physical activities, there are pool and ping pong tables and a library stocked with several thousand paperback volumes, a good number of them of the true crime variety. In one side office sit three acoustic guitars that inmates can strum. But, laughs one of the guards, no lessons for the inmates.

This is part of what endears the jail most to its residents — there is always something to do. Unlike federal penitentiaries like Joyceville or Millhaven where inmates are often locked in their cells for 23 hours of each day, the Rideau Correctional and Treatment Centre provides both work and educational opportunities along with recreation for its wards.

There are high school and life management classes that are taught during the day and a trade school where an inmate can learn carpentry or small engine repair. At the treatment centre, inmates can learn more dramatic life skills: how to stop from beating your wife or how to deaden that longing for alcohol or cheap crack cocaine.

To further pass the time, all inmates work, perhaps in the jail's kitchen or laundry. Those most trusted by administration are given an even greater privilege: the right to leave behind the 10-metre fences each day and work the land on the 500-acre provincially owned farm that sits adjacent to the jail. It is tiring, but productive, work. There are 400 head of cattle, fields of vegetables to supply the jail's kitchen and there even used to be some pigs.

The chickens are something else all together. Each year the farm produces about 50,000 dozen eggs, enough to supply every provincial institution east of Toronto. The chickens are kept in long rows of steel cages and many an inmate has professed to share an understanding of what the captive poultry must endure.

In return for the hard work in the fields or laundry, inmates are given a salary of $5 a week. Not much, but it goes into the inmate's canteen each week and enables him to buy extra supplies to make his time on the inside a little easier.

The canteen works much like a catalogue firm. Friends or families put money in the prisoners' accounts to help supplement their jail income. Every Monday the order form goes around and inmates are given the opportunity to buy cigarettes, a candy bar or maybe even a bar of Irish Spring so they won't be stuck with the coarse institution soap. Thursdays are a good day on the inside, because that's the day the inmates receive their order. And prices aren't that bad. A pack of 20 du Maurier costs $3.09, with tax included. A bag of Hostess All-Dressed chips will go for $0.79 and the magazines, whether it be *People*, *GQ* or *The National Enquirer*, are sold at cover price and are good for whiling away the evening hours.

As another diversion, the men are also given periodic rewards such as Fun Day, an event every August that matches dormitories in events like Tug of War and 100-metre dash. While some look down on the event as childish, by the time July has come around, bets are already being placed on the outcomes of the events and the victors will have bragging rights well into autumn.

Inmates can also access the forbidden fruits, whether it's a copy of *Hustler* or a pint of Jim Beam.

Like prisons around the world, thc bars and fences don't stop the flow of contraband. If you know the right people inside and have enough money, you get almost anything, including illicit drugs like hash and speed.

There are the downsides, of course. In an environment of so many men, it becomes necessary to test one's manhood. There are usually a couple of fist fights a week and the jail's nurses treat an abnormal number of scrapes, cuts and bruises that are the results of "accidental falls." If you do something really dumb, like get caught stealing from another inmate, it will be much more severe. A beating with a "sock lock" is the favoured punishment. Each inmate is given a combination lock so they can secure their valuables in steel boxes along one wall of the dorm. Placed in one of the white, institution socks and swung, it makes a formidable weapon.

There is also the 10-metre-high chain-link fence that surrounds the institution, a constant reminder that one's right to freedom has been temporarily suspended. Even more eerie are the spots on the fences, every one or two hundred yards and mostly at corners, where huge spools of razor wire adorn the top of the fence. These are the spots where in the past, prisoners have escaped. In one of the most recent cases, a young man serving 12 months for an attempted armed robbery at the Bank of Nova Scotia had requested a temporary pass so he could be with his girlfriend when she delivered the couple's second child. The pass was refused because the man had been in a few altercations, but that was no obstacle for him. One night he scaled the fence and disappeared into the woods. The Ottawa-Carleton police picked him up two days later at his girlfriend's apartment. He was the proud father of baby girl and had another six months added onto his sentence.

The men's movement is also limited within the jail. During the day, they pretty much have the run of the place. But at night it's a different story.

They are locked in their dorms between 10 p.m. and 6:30 a.m, and all the lights are shut down at 11 p.m. But the television can be kept on after that, and on weekends, well, the guys can pretty much stay up as late as they want, watching movies or sports and playing cards. Like most of the real world, no one has to work on Saturdays or Sundays.

Another one of the things that is hard for most men to handle is the lack of physical intimacy. Unlike federal prisons, the provincially run Rideau Treatment and Correctional Centre does not offer its inmates the chance for conjugal visits with their wives. Even during visits, which take place in a little room with 12 small tables and two guards, the guests' hands must always be kept on the table to avoid any indecent contact.

Still, despite the fences and the rules, the inmates who are there know how lucky they are. As the jail's superintendent says, nobody wants to serve their time anywhere else.

It is a system designed to help reform people who are going to return to the community in a matter of 12 or 16 months, men who can't be locked up and forgotten about. They try to treat their inmates as people, not animals, so when they do move in next door to you, they will be prepared to act in a civilized manner.

So with the late summer sun just starting to warm up the day, on the morning of Monday, September 30, 1996, the Rideau Correctional and Treatment Centre became the new home of the Champagne Gang.

Kevin, Marc, Yves and Tyler did not complain. They knew how lucky they were.

Y Y Y

"Hey. Hey buddy."

Kevin looked up from his bunk. Before him stood a slim youth, maybe 19, 20 tops. He had a wispy black mustache and a bad hockey haircut. He was dressed in the same rough, blue cotton outfit that all the inmates wore. Kevin recognized him as John, a punk kid who had a bed on the opposite end of the dorm from him. The word was he was doing time for assault after a vicious bar fight in Smiths Falls. He and some guy had been arguing over who was next on the pool table when the guy shoved John. John took his quart of Blue and smashed it into the guy's head. The guy received 39 stitches. John received nine months at Rideau Correctional. That was the word, anyway. You just didn't ask when you were on the inside.

"What?" Kevin growled.

John held out a copy of the *Ottawa Citizen*. On the cover was photos of him, Yves, Marc and Tyler and a feature story detailing their crimes. "Uhh, can you, like, sign this?" he quickly mumbled.

Kevin laughed. It had been like that ever since the newspapers starting covering their story. First it was in the *Ottawa Sun*, the local tabloid, with huge splashy headlines about the Champagne gang and their exorbitant lifestyles. Then a full-out feature in the *Citizen*. Now he heard that the story had been carried in newspapers around the country, from the *Edmonton Journal* to the *Montreal Gazette* and every small paper in between. It seemed everybody knew about them, at least everybody inside the jail.

"Look, that's all garbage. We're nothing special." Kevin turned back to the blue hard-covered book he was reading, a biography of the guys from New Brunswick who had started the McCain french fry company.

John stayed where he was. "Yeah, I know, but, it's like, I just want to show my friends when I get out, you know. Show them the guys I did time with."

Kevin rolled over and grabbed the pen. He quickly signed the paper and John hurried away, making sure none of the other inmates had witnessed the scene.

In truth, Kevin didn't really mind the attention. None of the guys did. It was flattering. Yves was especially thrilled with it. He had grown up idolizing Paddy Mitchell, the leader of the Stop Watch Gang. Mitchell's gang had hit dozens of banks over the years and taken in millions of dollars. Mitchell was also from Ottawa and had gained fame for his debonair ways and precision planning of bank jobs. He worked for more than 20 years before being caught and was always in the newspapers. Now, Yves figured he was in the same league, if not quite the same ballpark, as Paddy Mitchell. Hell,

Mitchell had even been popped for his robberies on Yves's birthday. If that wasn't a sign, what was?

And there was a material benefit to all the media attention as well. All the coverage had given them a reputation and it was definitely easy living inside with a reputation. Guys were a little slower to pick a fight, a bit more respectful when it came to splitting up work duties. In the world of crime, they'd risen to the status of celebrities.

The gang's reputation and, even more so, the fact that they were in the new jail, made life a lot better for the guys.

Rideau Correctional was a vast improvement over the Innes Road jail in Ottawa where they had been staying since June. That place was a zoo, a holding tank for everyone from young offenders who had boosted one too many cars to guys waiting to go to trial on first degree murder charges. Holiday Innes, as it was called, was no fucking holiday. There were fights every day, and even though the place was air-conditioned, it always stunk of sweat during the summer. The worst was the last three weeks, after the trial and the sentence, knowing they were going to Rideau Correctional but waiting for the transfer papers to go through. The days ground by with teeth-wearing tension as the guys waited for the wheels of bureaucracy to start to turn. It was a like a celebration when they were finally loaded into the gray vans for the drive out to the country.

The crew had been at Rideau for two months now and it had been an easy ride. Like Romper Room, Yves liked to crack.

Tyler was in the same dorm as Kevin, but Marc and Yves were in two separate dorms. To no one's surprise, with the mouths on both of them, Marc and Yves had already gotten in scuffles. Nothing major, just ego stuff. No one had touched Tyler or Kevin.

Kevin was already enrolled in treatment. He was going to Lifestyles class everyday. It was mind stuff, where the lady tried to teach you the difference between anti-social and pro-social behaviour and how to overcome anti-social tendencies. You had to talk a lot and fill out all these questionnaires. It was garbage really and Kevin felt like a bit of a patsy attending. But everyone told him it would look good when parole time came.

"Keep with it," Sylvie would say every night on the phone. "It'll show them you're trying to change."

The Lifestyles course would last another couple of weeks and then it would be time for the Relapse class. This was for those with drinking or drug problems and Kevin had heard it was like a 12-step program. Fuck that. Kevin would do it, but just because he and the boys drank hard and smoked a lot of hash, it didn't mean they had a problem.

It was hypocritical anyway to be preaching that stuff inside the fence. It was easier to score good dope at the jail then it was on the street any day. With so many guys serving time for drug offences, the jail population was the most connected around. A discreet handshake in the visitors room would be enough to pass 20 grams of hash and if you were really good, you could pass a couple of hundred grams during a one-hour visit. With as many as 12 prisoners and 24 visitors in the visiting room at any given time, there was no way the two guards on duty could watch everybody closely. Still, the bulk of the drugs came from the guys who were working the farm. With 500 acres of land, it was impossible to keep track of all inmates who were working out there. If a guy was on a tractor doing a field and his friend had happened to plant a couple of bricks of hash where he was working, who would know?

Of course, the drugs cost more on the inside too. A gram of hash went for $30 instead of the $15 or so it sold for on the street. But with friends, family and lovers kicking money into the inmates' canteens every week, there were always people with enough cash to make the purchases.

Y Y Y

Thinking of drugs and the way a soft hash high would make the afternoon float away, Kevin climbed out of his bunk in search of Yves.

That guy was always connected to dope and always had a lot of money on the inside. Just last week he had taken a guy for $3,500 playing Crazy Eights. Kevin laughed when he thought about it. Yves had sharked the kid good, playing the first couple rounds like a fool, tossing the eights at all the wrong times. Then, boom, as soon as the big money started coming on the table, Yves cleaned up. Only in jail could you make $3,500 playing Crazy Eights. People were insane here, they'd bet on anything.

Yves didn't keep his gambling to the card games either. He was still making bets with one of the Ottawa bookies. He had an arrangement where he'd phone in the bets and his friend Eric would handle the money. He was up $5,000 right now, having won big on some late-season baseball games and the football games. Eric collected the winnings and made the deposits into Yves's canteen in discreet amounts that wouldn't raise suspicion among the guards, or screws, as everyone on the inside called them.

Even though he was still gambling, Yves was working at changing his image too, taking Lifestyles class along with Kevin. But he had been acting up, cracking jokes and talking during the classes. The counsellors loved him, but he had still been warned that if he acted up again, he'd be gone. That would definitely look bad at the Parole Board. Marc was in Relapse right now and would switch over to Lifestyles when Kevin and Yves finished their course.

Tyler was the only one who wasn't taking counselling, figuring it wasn't worth the advantage at parole time to endure the moronic preachings of the jail counsellors.

They all attended church though. That was easy; all they had to do was file into the white room in the counselling centre every Monday, the day the chaplain had time for a visit, and doze on the benches while the guy did his spiel. Those who attended got a wooden cross to hang around their neck, and even more important, the chaplain's testimony to the Parole Board that they had indeed found God and were looking to change their life around. Religion was a pretty good scam.

Kevin swung open the door to Yves's dorm and found him asleep on his bunk. The fucking guy. He was supposed to be working in the kitchen right now, but he had everybody there under his thumb. They would sign him in and cover for him while Yves jerked off all day. It was a sweet set up.

Kevin worked in the kitchen too, but on a different shift. And he actually showed up and did the work. Tyler and Marc had jobs in the jail's laundry, washing sheets and folding towels. It wasn't bad at all. The jail staff decided not to give the guys fence clearance — no surprise, considering the severity of their crimes — so they couldn't work the farm or other outside jobs. But none of the guys really cared.

Kevin didn't exactly relish the idea of breaking his back clearing fields all day. Not for a lousy $5 a week. The kitchen or laundry work was just fine.

"Get up, you lazy bastard." Kevin leaned over the bunk and slapped Yves in the face a couple of times. His eyes opened.

"What?" Yves was startled. He spun his head, still asleep, eyes open.

"Let's smoke."

Yves stretched out and rubbed his eyes before reaching under his mattress and pulling out his stash. They left his dorm and found Marc at the laundry, then cut outside behind one of the dormitories. Tyler was acting a bit flaky lately. He would still hang around with the guys, but was careful about it. He did not want to get any extra time added to his sentence for jailhouse offences.

As they walked, Marc started cursing. He was still pissed about his night class. Yves and Marc were taking high school credits at night school inside the jail to try and get their diplomas. Yves had signed up for two bird courses, How To Be A Successful Student and Nutrition. But Marc was in English and was writing an essay on Margaret Atwood's *The Edible Woman*.

"How can you fucking write in here with all these monkeys? There's too much noise and shit."

He watched as Yves rolled up the joint, lubed it then sparked it up. "I should have taken fucking nutrition. Canada Food Groups. How hard can that shit be?"

Yves inhaled deeply and tried to change the topic. "Did you talk to Wayne yet?" He passed the joint to Marc, who took a long drag, then nodded.

He had met Wayne last week. He was an older guy in his early 30s, tall and skinny with tattoos covering his back and chest, serving an 18-month bit in connection with a break-and-enter. Wayne owned an alarm company and in the spring of '95 had set up a system for a jewellery store in the east end of Ottawa. It was a top-of-the-line system, retailing for about $15,000 and *should* have completely protected the store against anything. That is, if Wayne had installed it properly. Wayne had "forgotten" to connect the wires that would trigger the alarm if there was movement in the store or if the door was broken open or if the safe was jimmied. It was a pretty big mistake. Especially when, for $25,000, he told a friend exactly how to beat the system.

Two weeks after Wayne installed the alarm, the store got stung for more than $250,000. The thief had pried open the back door and smashed each of the display cases to get the jewellery, then blown open the huge industrial safe where the cash was kept. Not a single alarm bell had rung.

Perhaps police would have accepted Wayne's "innocent mistake" theory, except that his police record showed several armed robberies and some outstanding warrants for fraud. Police were immediately suspicious. When officers caught his friend trying to pawn diamond necklaces, it was pretty much a done deal. Wayne's friend confessed everything and they were both convicted.

Marc and Wayne had shot a couple of games of pool together two days ago and Wayne had been talking the trade. He was amazed at how much Marc knew about doing safes and disarming alarms and had agreed to meet with them all next week to give them tips. Not that they were planning to go back to work once they got out of jail. But, as the authorities professed, education was a good thing. Anyway, it was a good way to kill time.

"Wayne says we can get together next weekend. We gotta bring the smoke."

Kevin and Yves nodded.

Marc took another drag on the joint and passed it over to Kevin and let his muscles relax as the hash began to work its magic. Little adventures with Wayne were important. Killing time was very important.

Even though it was a short sentence, the time was killing the guys, especially Kevin. And he was having problems falling asleep lately, seemingly adding seconds, minutes, hours to his stay. It was hard to sleep in the dorms. Guards passed every 30 minutes, setting off an electronic monitor that let off a high-pitched beep marking their progress. It was like an alarm clock. Even worse, during the night, all the main bathrooms were closed off, so anyone who had the urge had to use the metal toilet in the corner of the dorm. A guy with a big bladder could make that toilet sound like a goddamn cymbal factory.

If you started lying awake at night thinking about the ocean of time between you and your release date, it was suicide.

Under provincial legislation, inmates are not allowed to apply for parole until they have served one third of their sentences, an eight-month stretch in the gang's case. That meant the gang wouldn't be eligible until May of 1997, which was still another six long months away.

Once the one third of the sentence was up, the guys would get two shots at parole hearings. If they could convince the Parole Board they had been rehabilitated and deserved to be returned to the community, they could be on the street by the middle of May. If they were rejected in May, they could try again in August or September. If they failed both times — a situation no one even wanted to consider — then they'd have to serve until their statutory release, after two-thirds of their sentence expired. That meant they'd have to do 16 months and would be released in January 1998. Not a pleasant option. Technically, another eight months would remain on their sentence, but only a minuscule percentage of inmates actually served their entire sentence. That was reserved for offenders deemed dangerous and likely to re-offend and the Parole Board had to file for a special order to keep the offender behind bars after two-thirds of their sentence was up. With the cost of housing inmates and the overcrowding in prisons and jails, the system would collapse if all were forced to serve their full sentences. The Champagne Gang stood to benefit from the bloated system.

Kevin took a last drag off the roach and butted it against the wall. He ground the remains into tiny, innocent-looking pieces and tossed them into the wind.

It was almost time for Kevin's Lifestyles class and Marc had to get back to the laundry. Yves smiled that blissful look. He would stop by the kitchen to get a salad and a sandwich and make sure he wasn't missed.

Y Y Y

Kevin felt his stomach twist. Shit. He leaned over to Marc. "Fifteen minutes. Fifteen fucking minutes? I thought these things were supposed to take an hour. They must have killed him in there."

Marc and Kevin were waiting outside the meeting room at the admissions and discharge building. Inside the Parole Board was holding their hearings. Tyler had gone in 15 minutes ago. He had just been shown outside, his head down. He turned, shook his head and gave Kevin and Marc the thumbs down sign.

"Look," said Marc. "He didn't do the classes. We did the classes. Anyways, Tyler can be a headcase. We can still get it."

A stern-looking woman appeared at the door. "Flamini. Marc Flamini."

Marc stood up, straightened his blue prison uniform and winked at Kevin. This was it.

It was May 9, almost eight months after they had been sentenced and the first time they were eligible for parole. The three of them — Kevin, Marc and Tyler — had all applied for parole. Yves had decided to take a gamble and wait another couple of months. He figured there was absolutely no way they'd let him walk this early, so he was going to serve another two or three months, then try. It would look good at the hearing, that kind of modesty. Kevin could see that weasel Yves in the parole hearing.

"I just didn't feel I had done enough time for my offenses," Yves would say in his most apologetic voice. "I really wanted to pay my debt to society."

That little shit. And if Tyler's hearing had been any indication, Yves's gamble was going to pay off.

Damn. Kevin had worked hard to get his parole case in order. He got more than 30 letters of recommendation to present to the Parole Board, from family who said they'd give him a place to stay, friends as character witnesses, to guys who said they'd give him a job when he got out. He even had the support of staff at the Guelph Centre for Gambling Addiction. It was one of the leading gambling clinics in the country and Kevin had worked hard to get a bed there. They were going to accept him as soon as he got out.

Kevin knew he had a gambling problem. He figured he had lost more than $800,000 in the last four years by betting with bookies and on Pro-Line. He wanted help. He also wanted to look good at the Parole Board hearing and how could getting a bed at that clinic not look good?

Sylvie was waiting in the Visitor's Room, anxious as he was. She was going through hard times without him. She still had those conspiracy charges against her, there was no money left and bills were beginning to pile up. She couldn't work and the social assistance didn't go far. Kevin didn't even want to think about the credit card bills. It seemed she cried almost every night when they talked on phone. Kevin wanted to be there for her.

She was there for him. Only Sylvie and Marc's girlfriend, Terri Anne, were still waiting for them. Tania broke up with Yves in February and was already seeing another man, some chubby dipshit named Fred. Yves couldn't get over it; he could've accepted Tania leaving him for someone with a bit of class or style. But this Fred guy was once divorced and twice a loser. Hell, Yves told the guys over breakfast one time last month, if Tania had at least gone with someone decent, he could've had the pleasure of tracking him down and beating the shit out of him. Fred was so pathetic, he wasn't even worth the time.

Tyler got the bad word from Kerri just last week. That one wasn't as much of a surprise. Kerri was a beautiful woman and a good ride, but she was flighty. Tyler was kind of surprised she had stayed around as long as he did.

The girls who stuck around while their men were on the inside were the ones, figured Kevin, who were the real thing.

He checked the clock on the wall. Forty-five minutes had passed. That was a very good sign. Without thinking, he knocked on the wall, just like old times.

The screws would die if he got parole. It seemed almost every guard in the joint gave the guys a hard time. What with the media coverage, the attention they got from the other inmates and the mouths on Yves and Marc, they were probably the most reviled guys in the jail from an administration standpoint. Kevin laughed to himself. Maybe they would be so eager to be rid of him, they'd give him parole.

The door opened. Marc was being led out. He shrugged, then held two fingers about an inch apart. He had been rejected. But not by much.

"Grandmaison. Kevin Grandmaison."

Kevin stood up. If Marc had just barely been rejected, he had a good shot. Marc had more misconducts, Marc didn't have as many letters of support, Marc wasn't checking himself into a gambling clinic.

And let's face it, thought Kevin, Marc could be a bigger asshole than he was.

He walked into the room and sat before the panel of three men and two women. He was ready for their questions.

Y Y Y

"I told you. No chance. You shoulda been smart like me. Fuuuuuccccccck."

Yves was sitting and gloating on a bunk while Tyler, Marc and Kevin sat at a table playing cards. He hadn't stopped giving it to them since they had all been rejected for parole.

Marc and Tyler had sloughed it off, but Kevin was starting to get pissed. He thought he was going to get it. The Board wanted to give it to him. They had even told him so. It was just his crimes were so high-profile, they feared the backlash if he got out early.

"I sincerely believe you're a changed man," said one of the women after the hearing. "But you must understand. We have to consider the perception. It would not be good."

What would it look like? they argued. The man who orchestrated *at least* 54 break-and-enters that netted $1.5 million walking after a lousy eight months. It would look bad. Kevin had smiled to himself. They kept on bringing up the 54 jobs, the 54 victims, the 54 crimes. If only they had known the whole truth. If all the victims had really been counted, he wouldn't have even been at the Rideau Correctional and Treatment Centre. He would have been cooling his heels at a federal penitentiary. Still, they complimented him on seeking treatment for his gambling addiction and acknowledged there was tremendous support for him in the community. Just wait three or four months, they promised. You'll get it for sure after the summer.

Kevin had managed to shake their hands, but he was deflated. He wasn't sure what to do now.

After being rejected, Marc, Kevin and Tyler had one more appeal for parole, at a time they chose before the next eight months was up. Based on what the Parole Board had said to Kevin, they all figured they would have a pretty good shot in September. Yves was cocky now, but Marc and Kevin were positive Yves would get rejected the first time too, the loudmouth. And for the rest, there was no way the Board could justify letting one of the gang out before the others.

Now they had to decide if they would even apply for parole again or did they just want to serve their second eight months and simply walk away?

The problem with parole was that it would be absolutely loaded with conditions. Ugly ones. They would all face curfews of 11 p.m. at night and would have to be in their own home between 11 p.m. and 6:30 the next morning. They would have to report to a parole officer and would constantly be monitored. And there would be a clause that no one could leave the Ottawa-Carleton region.

The most dangerous thing about parole was the non-association clause. It would be exactly the same as the one on their probation order — the guys simply couldn't be with each other — but the consequences were much more serious. If they got caught together while on probation, they would be reprimanded and at most, serve another 30-day stint. But if they got caught together while out on parole, it would be a violation of parole, back to jail to complete the original sentence *and* up to another year added onto their sentence.

So their dilemma was, should they try to be released in September and face those kind of restrictions? Or should they just wait an extra four months and get the greater freedom that came with statutory release?

"I don't want them having nothing on me," Marc argued, putting in his bid to convince the others to do the whole stretch.

It was early June now, so they still had a couple of months to consider their decision. Their time had gotten easier as they got used to the routines and the rhythms of the jail. They watched a lot of television and spent a lot of time playing floor hockey. They were also devouring the books in the library, mostly the true crime ones. Yves had already read books about a gang who had ripped off hotels in the States, a gang of police officers who had done a bank job for $22.5 million and was working his way through the book on Paddy Mitchell for the fourth time. The books gave him ideas, and he liked to see how the four of them stacked up.

Kevin had just won the hand of gin and was dealing another. "Yves, you fucking headcase. Why don't you get off your ass and play. And shut up about parole already."

Yves shrugged and jumped down from the bunk. "I'm going to get some soup first." He reached into his locker and grabbed a Lipton Cup of Soup and then went to get the bug. Every dorm had a "bug" to heat up the soup. Technically they were illegal and if the guards found them, they'd be confiscated. But how the hell did they think they warmed up their soup? The "bug" was just the end of an extension cord, cut off. You plug it in, dip the end in the soup and waited for the soup to start to steam. Better than a microwave. Yves got his chicken soup going and joined the others at the card table.

Kevin was right. It was no good talking about parole. It just made you long for the outside. And they all had big plans for when they got out.

First there were the plans they had so earnestly listed on the parole applications and spoke about to the guards and their families.

Marc was going to wait tables or tend bar in the Byward Market in downtown Ottawa. He was tight with most of the big-shot restaurant and bar owners in the Market, having dropped tens of thousands of dollars in their establishments wining and dining women. They'd hook him up with a job, no problem. He would also move back in with Terri Anne and start saving money, he promised the parole board. He was going to open his own restaurant one day. He had lots of time. He would be only 24 years old when released.

Kevin was going to register for a business program at Algonquin College, try to get a job some place where his past wouldn't be a problem. He was a little worried about being hired. Facts are facts: no real job experience, and after all, he'd be turning 30 this fall. How many employers were looking for 30-year-olds with little education and a criminal record? First though, there was that month in the Guelph gambling clinic and then he'd be back with Sylvie, trying to get their life in order.

Tyler still dreamed of the test shot he had with the Toronto modelling agency. He would love to get into television, maybe as a broadcaster, maybe on a TV show. He had the looks, everyone said so. His mom lived in Ottawa and would take him in, giving him time to get back on his feet. And if nothing else, he could always go back to Carleton University and finish his degree. He'd only be 26 years old. Lots of time to start a new life.

Yves planned to tell the parole board he would go to night school to finish his high school education and then, maybe, join his uncle in the landscaping business. If not, he could go to Algonquin with Kevin and maybe take a course in computers. Who knew?

Those were the plans. At least the ones they told the parole board about. Finances would be tight. They wouldn't be earning $3,000 or $4,000 a week anymore. They would have to face the reality of trying to make do on $300 or $400 a week when they first got out.

But they weren't worried. They had a safety net. The Proceeds of Crime Unit never came after them. The police recovered about $30,000 worth of stamps at the time of the arrests, but nothing else. They guys didn't have money in the bank, so the OPP didn't bother to go after them to get back what was stolen.

But that didn't mean the guys were broke. Both Marc and Tyler had wardrobes that would cost more than $50,000 if bought new. Kevin had a home gym, including a treadmill and StairMaster, that would be priced at $20,000 in most fitness shops. All four had high-end furniture, from 27-inch colour TVs to $1,200 coffee tables, in storage and waiting to furnish their new digs when they returned to the real world.

And even after all the gambling, the partying, the vacations and the drinking, there might even have been a bit of money left over.

None would admit to it of course. Each of them had told the police that they would be destitute upon leaving jail.

But when Marc leaned back in the visiting room and winked about his "not being stupid" with all of his money or Yves boasted of the gang's plan to return to Acapulco for a month upon release to try and shake their pasty complexions and rejuvenate their once-glorious tans, it was obvious they did not plan to be paupers.

Not when they left jail.

Not when they reached middle age.

Not ever.

Epilogue

In what seemed like a gift from above, by the first week of July 1997, Kevin, Yves, Marc and Tyler had received fence clearance at the Rideau Correctional and Treatment Centre. This meant instead of working in the cramped kitchen or steamy laundry, they were free to work outside on the farm.

All four of them were assigned to the chicken barn. In the mornings they swept the barn free of droppings and collected any eggs the hens had laid during the night. After lunch, they spread bucket after bucket of chicken feed and made whatever repairs were needed to the chicken coops.

It was good, physical work and opened their eyes to things they had never seen before. One day, Kevin watched a cow give birth in an adjoining barn, even helped as the workers had to pull the calf from its mother's womb. On that same day, he saw a hen rupture itself while it tried to pass an egg, an event he told Sylvie about on the phone that evening with awe and disgust.

The best part of working on the farm was the breaks. All four were in such good shape that they could complete their day's work in half the allotted time. That meant every day they could spend several hours lounging on the picnic tables, smoking hash and letting the summer sun darken their skin. It almost made jail life bearable.

Yves was also going through a fair bit of ribbing at this time. His gamble had failed. Even though he waited an extra eight weeks to apply for parole, the board had no mercy and he was quickly rejected. While Yves moped about it for a while, it provided endless laughs for Kevin, Marc and Tyler as they all lay out beneath the hot sun.

It was during these heady days in early July that Kevin was called to the visiting room. It was a call that confused him. Inmates were only allowed one visit a week and Sylvie had already been up, so who could this be?

His instincts told him it couldn't be any good. His instincts were right.

It was two officers from the Gatineau police, a Quebec town across the Ottawa River from Ottawa, and they had a few questions for Kevin. It so happened that there had been a spate of rooftop break-ins at grocery and drug stores in recent years, crimes that had gone completely unsolved.

However, the police did keep all the evidence from the crime scenes, including a set of tools — a crowbar, a pickaxe and screwdrivers — left behind at one store during a hasty exit. These tools still had their price tags and bar codes on them, so the Gatineau police were quickly able to determine that they had been bought at a Canadian Tire in Ottawa one day in 1995. The Gatineau police also had copies of Kevin's confession, in which he admitted to buying similar tools at that same Canadian Tire on the same day and using them for a job in Peterborough.

What a coincidence.

And of course, in the deal Kevin and the rest of the gang had signed with the Crown Attorney's office, they had received immunity for any other crimes they may have committed in Ontario and British Columbia. Not Quebec.

The officers left, promising to investigate further. Kevin returned to the chicken farm, shaken.

The next day, Kevin was called back to the visiting room. This time he prepared himself for the worst, completely expecting another meeting with the Gatineau police. Instead, it was the Aylmer police, another Quebec town just up the highway from Gatineau.

They too had a spate of rooftop break-ins that remained unsolved, and same as in Gatineau, they had no suspects. The Aylmer force had talked to the Gatineau cops the day before and had been advised it might be worth their time to question Kevin. Now Kevin was worried and so were the other three. He got on the phone that night and arranged to get a Quebec lawyer to look into the case.

It took a week to get to the bottom of it, a week in which Kevin slept very poorly. It turned out Kevin was a suspect in about a dozen break-and-enters in western Quebec. They had little evidence and weren't all that keen to spend the money they needed to get more. There was also nothing to connect the crimes to anyone else in the gang. The police were ready to offer Kevin a sweet deal: admit to everything he had done in their jurisdictions, which would allow the Aylmer and Gatineau police to close the files on the cases, and the police wouldn't lay any additional charges against Kevin.

Kevin was quite pleased.

As July wore on, the police and Kevin's lawyer worked out the final details of the agreement while Kevin spent his days on the chicken farm. Everyone expected it to be a done deal by the middle of August, a deal that would not affect his statutory release date in January.

Raking chicken shit in the hot July sun, Kevin couldn't help but laugh. Despite his circumstances — he was broke, in jail and had a criminal record — things could be much worse. He had been very lucky on the Quebec deal; in fact, he had been lucky on both deals. With his unconditional release coming up fast, starting life again, starting life right, Kevin Grandmaison couldn't help but think he was a very lucky man.

Appendix I

The following stores were the targets of break-and-enters that Kevin Grandmaison, Yves Belanger, Marc Flamini and Tyler Wilson formally admitted to committing. When they pled guilty to these crimes, they were granted immunity for any other break-and-enters they may have committed in the provinces of Ontario or British Columbia.

Although there are only 54 jobs admitted as evidence in court, the officers involved in the cases suspect that the four men were involved in more than 200 break-and-enters across Canada.

Zellers Department Store
275 Brockville Street
Smiths Falls, Ontario

Loeb I.G.A. Food Store
110 Lansdowne Avenue
Carleton Place, Ontario

Shefield and Sons
1154 Chemong Road
Peterborough, Ontario

K-Mart Department Store
226 Dundas Street East
Trenton, Ontario

Woolco Department Store
RR#5
Woodstock, Ontario

Consumers Distributing
1670 Heron Road
Ottawa, Ontario

Bingo Country
1382 Weber Street East
Kitchener, Ontario

Consumers Distributing
331 King George Road
Brantford, Ontario

Beaver Lumber
2435 Princess Street
Kingston, Ontario

Beaver Lumber
64 King Street East
Oshawa, Ontario

Top Rank Bingo Hall
1735 Bailey Street
Pickering, Ontario

Rave Convenience Store
1300 King Street East
Oshawa, Ontario

Peter's Pantry Restaurant (2X)
1394 Richmond Road
Ottawa, Ontario

Valu Mart Food Store
350 Victoria Street North
Tweed, Ontario

Bingo Country
884 Division Street
Cobourg, Ontario

Shoppers Drug Mart
466 Gardiners Road
Kingston, Ontario

Pharma Plus Drug Store
2685 Iris Avenue
Ottawa, Ontario

Shoppers Drug Mart
300 Bath Road
Kingston, Ontario

Bingo Country
806 Chelsea Street
Brockville, Ontario

Loeb Food Store
1225 Princess Street
Kingston, Ontario

K-Mart Department Store
600 Bath Road
Kingston, Ontario

Canadian Tire Store
1333 Wilson Road North
Oshawa, Ontario

Electronic Boutique
390 North Front Street
Belleville, Ontario

Pier One Imports
22 Stephenson Road South
Oshawa, Ontario

Shoppers Drug Mart
416 St. Clair Street
Chatham, Ontario

Pharma Plus Drug Store
401 Kent Street West
Lindsay, Ontario

Big V Drug Store
865 Chemong Road
Peterborough, Ontario

Hallmark Card and Postal Outlet
925 Ontario Street
Stratford, Ontario

Pharma Plus Drug Store
1067 Ontario Street
Stratford, Ontario

Shoppers Drug Mart
550 King Street North
Waterloo, Ontario

Pharma Plus Drug Store
Unit 62 - 1380 London Road
Sarnia, Ontario

Groombridge Sampler Outlet
Unit 31 - 1380 London Road
Sarnia, Ontario

Shoppers Drug Mart
355 Hespler Road
Cambridge, Ontario

Big V Drug Store
500 Grantham, Ontario
St. Catharines, Ontario

Big V Drug Store
484 Plains Road East
Burlington, Ontario

Dell Pharmacy
54 Wilson Street
Ancaster, Ontario

Big V Drug Store
56 Wilson Street
Ancaster, Ontario

Shoppers Drug Mart
34 Plaza Drive
Dundas, Ontario

Shoppers Drug Mart
1355 Kingston Road
Pickering, Ontario

The Gallery
84 Lynden Road
Brantford, Ontario

Shoppers Drug Mart
686 Queenston Road
Hamilton, Ontario

Shoppers Drug Mart
1515 Rebecca Street
Oakville, Ontario

Shoppers Drug Mart
1865 Lakeshore Road West
Mississauga, Ontario

Shoppers Drug Mart
769 Southdale Road East
London, Ontario

Shoppers Drug Mart
360 Cardoc Street South
Strathroy, Ontario

Shoppers Drug Mart
4 - 17 Holland Street
St. Thomas, Ontario

Shoppers Drug Mart
3575 Douglas Street
Saanich, British Columbia

Shoppers Drug Mart
420 Hazeldean Road
Kanata, Ontario

Shoppers Drug Mart
2015 Long Lake Road
Sudbury, Ontario

Shoppers Drug Mart
1642 Merivale Road
Nepean, Ontario

Shoppers Drug Mart
1300 King Street East
Oshawa, Ontario

Shoppers Drug Mart
70 Front Street
Orillia, Ontario

Shoppers Drug Mart
210 Glenridge Avenue
St. Catharines, Ontario

In July 1997, police officers representing the Quebec communities of Gatineau and Aylmer came to the Rideau Correctional and Treatment Centre to talk with Kevin Grandmaison.

They had evidence that he had been involved in several break-ins in Quebec. Grandmaison cut a deal where he would admit to all their crimes but would receive no additional time in jail.